Two Rare Birds
A Legacy of Love
Stories of Life, Death, Courage & Purpose

Lily Myers Kaplan

ISBN: 1493740393
ISBN 13: 9781493740390
Library of Congress Control Number: 2013921596
CreateSpace Independent Publishing Platform, North Charleston, South Carolina

Praise for Two Rare Birds: A Legacy of Love

Lily Myers Kaplan's memoir, written with an unsentimental devotion to truth, is a guide through the underworld of loss and into the chamber of renewal. It is a testament to love and an enduring statement of fidelity to what matters most in life. By leading us through the great hall of sorrows Lily enables us to find the courage to discover who we really are, where we belong, and what is sacred. This book is a lantern in the dark. Read it and find heart.

Francis Weller
Author of ***Entering the Healing Ground: Grief, Ritual and the Soul of the World***

Two Rare Birds is an enchanting story of love, grief and wisdom that deeply moves the heart in unexpected ways. The spiritual transformation that is potential in the journey with cancer and the encounter with death is illuminated in these pages. Let Lily Myers Kaplan's words inspire you to realize the compassion that you are.

Dale Borglum
Executive Director of ***The Living/Dying Project***

I found Two Rare Birds profoundly personal, compelling and inspirational. As the characters grappled with their dark nights, I came face to face with my own soul and found an expanded and deepened understanding of my mortality. Rich in imagery, Two Rare Birds speaks a universal language, making it accessible and relevant to all.

Julie Adams Church
Author of ***Uncommon Friends: Celebrating the Human-Animal Bond***

In today's world, too often flooded with cynicism and unrest, Lily Myers Kaplan's Two Rare Birds – A Legacy of Love *offers an important source to heal your troubled soul. Each pate of delicious and lyrical prose is a generous gift as you ponder life's deepest questions. A timely and important book.*

Jim Conlon
Author of ten books, including: ***At the Edge of Our Longing: Unspoken Hunger for Sacredness*** as well as ***Depth and Beauty, Wonder and Belonging: A Book of Hours for the Monastery of the Cosmos***

Two Rare Bird is heartbreaking and uplifting...an inspiring story of love and hope. A slam-dunk for those with Pema Chodron or Cheryl Strayed on their night tables.

Marcy Baskin
Author of ***Assisted Living: Questions I Wish I Had Asked***
Founder of **Elder Roads**

COVER PHOTO: After choosing this photograph for the cover I learned that these beautiful birds are Ibis. Revered in Ancient Egypt as a sacred Deity, the Ibis is known for bestowing all arts and sciences unto mankind. Commonly referred to as Thoth, this God was recognized for his wisdom, honored as a great magician and revered as a guide to the afterlife. What a fitting image for *Two Rare Birds: A Legacy of Love!*

PHOTO CREDITS:

<u>Photo taken by John W. Bederman:</u> "To capture a moment in time gives me great joy, yet seeing others react to it is even greater, one of life's little pleasures that makes my day."

<u>Photo Enhancements by Fred Kaplan,</u> documentary filmmaker and still photographer, whose fascination with the interplay of light and shadow is revealed through the often overlooked, common beauty of life.

Dedication

To Dave and Lois,
whose spirits live on,
shining brightly
in our hearts.

Table of Contents

Foreword xiii

Prologue: From Whence I Came. xv

Section One: The Descent 1

    One: Who Am I?. 3

Shattered; The Quest Begins Anew; Three Sisters; The Magothy; The Brick House; Myers Restaurant; The Heritage House; The Temple of Milrace; Ye Olde English Pub; Ad-ventcha!; Mourning as My Path

    Two: Being Human 27

The Paradox of Me and Lo; Love and Betrayal; Moving on to Hawk Mountain; Relationship Mirrors; The Pedestal Crumbles; Wisdom of the Body; The Green-Eyed Monster; Truce

Three: Life Is a Schoolroom 53

Falling in Love; Dave, Dave, Dave; The Thirteenth Fairy; Truth Time; The Dream; Cancer Ping-Pong; Relay for Life

Section Two: Deepening into Destiny 77

Four: The Search 79

A Roller Coaster of Love; Paradise Lost Is Consciousness Gained; Remember; God? The Voice of the Skeptic; Seer

Five: Practice, Practice, Practice 95

The Triumvirate; Oy! Is Just One Part of Joy; Vigil One - Vigil Two - Vigil Three; Let's Do It!; Two Eggs in a Nest

Six: A Year to Surrender 117

Camp; Memorial Day Number Three; Service and Surrender; Celebration and the Big Scoop; The White Flag of Surrender; Patience of a Saint; Love, Healing, and Purpose; The Dark of the Night; The Dark of the Night Redux

Section Three: Discovering Grace 145

Seven: Three Good-Byes 147

The Fire Blazes; Lambchops; The Sun at My Feet; Free to Soar; Lojo Loses her Mojo; Taking Matters into her Own

Hands; Labor; Cleansing Rituals; Celebration of Life;
The Frio; Wholehearted Love; Transitions

Eight: Ancestor Speaking 183
The Frozen Waterfall; Visitation on the Snake River;
Return to Circle; Signs of Spirit; Ashes to Ashes; Red
Mesa; Rainbow Bridge; Giant Butterfly; Crying for a
Vision; The Blue Pearl

Nine: Legacy 211
One Thread; Completing the Clan Wave; Spirit of Resh;
Manifestation; Carrying On

Epilogue: Sitting Shiva 221

Foreword

Dear Reader,

I want you to know that this story, *Two Rare Birds*, is real and true. I am Lily's sister, Sally. In a few short years our close knit family of seven shrank to just three. That left me, along with Lily and her husband Seth, to navigate the murky waters of our grief. *Two Rare Birds* tells how the heartbreak of our losses triggered questions, realizations and profound Love.

I know this story is the real deal because I lived it. And though *Two Rare Birds* is Lily's story, it is mine too. I believe we could all claim it as our own. Every one of us has experienced loss—possibly through death, divorce, illness or decline. We each die many deaths in one lifetime. We die to childhood and enter adolescence, then die to adolescence as we become adults, and we die to relationships and start new ones. Our familiar lives change and in each death is the potential for a richer life.

Though I may long for the way it *used to be*, I also know that change is inevitable. *Two Rare Birds* re-counts a roller coaster—a series of events—in which healing is born from the unwelcome, unforeseen, and bewildering illnesses and eventual deaths of our beloved family. But this book is much more than an account of death and grief. It is a heart opening story that shows how personal struggle and overwhelming sadness can give way to remarkable growth.

Two Rare Birds invites us to engage in the bigger story of Life and learning, beyond the visible and the obvious, where we may experience the Love that underlies it all. And so, dear reader, I invite you into our family and into the story of our Two Rare Birds. Much love,

Sally

Prologue: From Whence I Came

Years ago, my parents put together a small photo album and titled it "From Whence You Came." Many of those pictures—grandparents, great-grandparents, and the great-greats (including aunts, uncles, cousins, and colleagues)—sit on an altar above my desk where I write. Though they live in the invisible ancestral lands, I honor them in the way of indigenous people, offering favorite foods, water, and flowers now and again. Since neither my two siblings nor I have children, our clan line is ending. The forces of our entire lineages are being expressed in a final burst through the three of us, like the prolific flowering of fruit just before harvest. With such potency moving through me, I know that this is their book, along with mine.

As I write, I carry within me an image of a tribe. People are sitting around a glowing hearth at the center of a village. The circle is whole, filled with young adults and elders—some single, some coupled—along with flirtatious teens, babies, toddlers, and wild kids. All cycles of life are present. Stories are being told. These stories of history and mythology are the foundation of my tribe, the remaining essential substance of my people, and the soul of my village. By speaking the stories, I keep alive what has come and gone before me, reminding me of who I want to be…and more importantly, of who I was born to become.

Two Rare Birds: A Legacy of Love has become my personal myth, a feast of my clan's stories spiced with archetypal mythologies and cooked up over the fire at the hearth of my ancestral tribe. At first I thought of the book as a simple collage of stories about my sister, Lois, and her husband, Dave's cancer journey and their untimely deaths. But it has become so much more. Through telling their stories, I have come to know more truly who *I* am—a woman whose story includes love, betrayal, forgiveness, and death. But, beyond that, I am a woman whose legacy rests upon the backs of her ancestors. Writing *Two Rare Birds* has taken me all the way back to the beginning…

Section One

The Descent

I can no longer watch from a safe distance as someone else faces a battle with a cancer. My own fears will arise. My resolve to come through this as a whole person will be tested. My own faith in the One much greater than me—greater than the cancer—will be challenged.

I believe this is something everyone must face before we reunite with our Beloved…the challenges simply come to us in different forms.

—Dave

One

Who Am I?

Be one
Be all of you
Be yourself
Be be be

Search for the one
Search for all of you
Search for yourself
Search search search

Find the One
Find all of you
Find yourself
Find find find

Be, Search, Find
All within your heart
One, you, yourself
All the same

—Lois

Shattered

When my sister Lois died three years ago (and her husband, Dave, nine months later) the world fell out from under me. I had no idea who I was anymore. Never mind that my mother had died just three months before or my father a couple of years before that. With Lois gone, the foundation of who I knew myself to be was yanked from under my feet, dropping me right down to my knees—where I stayed for an entire year. Months after her passing, on my one day of freedom from the demands of directing Oakland Feather River Family Camp, I'd suddenly descend into sheer wailing, as if on cue. Driving through wildflower laden, rushing snow-melt-filled mountain passes, my car, a bubble of deepest privacy, is where my grief found its most holy expression. The rainbow-colored basket into which I'd nestled the tiny stuffed bear with lifelike, moveable arms and legs—one of Lo's prized possessions—hung from the rearview mirror. It bounced down the country roads with me as I mourned my sister—and my lost self. Among the balsam scent of 150-foot pines, tucked on a sunny spit of sand beside a crystal mountain lake, I cried and ranted and slept and let my heart break. *Who would I be in a world without a Lois in it?* I wondered. I had no idea.

To say my relationship with Lois was complicated is an understatement. That we loved each other profoundly and hurt one another deeply is also without question. The fabric of our sisterhood reached far beyond the conflicts of ordinary sibling rivalry; we were entangled by love and betrayal, the raw material of a most beautiful and wrenching intimacy—the lead that became the alchemist's

4

gold. Lois had forever been a steady fixture in my world. As my Big Sister, she was someone I'd looked up to and tried to emulate. Through the tumult of our relationship, I'd discovered who I was and wasn't. Without her living and breathing body to push up against, I no longer walked through the world in the same way, feeling, instead, as if my sense of wholeness and ease had died with her. Ushering my sister across the threshold of life and death blew me completely apart.

The Quest Begins Anew

I thought I knew who I was, but after losing Lois I felt like Inanna, of the ancient Sumerian myth, who traveled to the underworld to support her sister Ereshkigal. In a jealous rage, Ereshkigal stripped Inanna of her garments, symbols of her outer self. I was also being stripped of my outer identities. Ereshkigal hung Inanna on a hook to rot, and I, too, felt like a piece of raw meat, unrecognizable to myself. I no longer knew myself as a soul coach or director of a camp, or even as steward of a piece of Sierra mountain land I'd come to know like the territory of my own body. I simply could not identify with any of it, nor with any of the roles I'd held to date. No kind of *doing* animated me anymore. Inanna, dangling from a hook in the underworld, was dying a symbolic death—a dark winter of the soul. Like her, I entered a period of darkness, dying to my former self. Though I'd visited the cocoon-like underworld of my deep psyche before, *nothing* had prepared me for entry into the darkness of unknowing I encountered once Lois took her last breath. But if I learned anything from my sister's death, it is that my internal world and the one surrounding me are ever-evolving, ever-initiating places. I hung on the metaphorical hook, trying to discover my place in the cosmos, my purpose in the universe, and my work in the world while rotting away what was no longer true to my real self. It turned out that mourning my Big Sister became a journey of the soul I had no choice but to make.

I've wanted to understand who *I am* for as long as I can remember. When I was about three years old and sharing a room with Lois, I had a glimpse of the numinous—a peek into the realm of the eternal—which is still alive in me, as if it happened yesterday. I'd awakened early one morning, where, from my bed, I could see that the maple tree outside my window had miraculously burst into the most light-filled, stunning, magnificent spring green. Beyond the eruption of leaves, I felt, more than saw, a soft light emanating from the tree, surrounding everything in its sphere, including me. Back then, I did not have words for the experience. Even now, though I can see the aura and exquisite color in my mind's eye, I struggle to find words for that touch of the ephemeral. New leaves burst open on branches that had been completely bare only a day before; it seemed like a miracle. For just a moment, I basked in the timeless glow. Then the radiance faded, and the tree—and I along with it—became ordinary again. This is my earliest memory of awe. I soon started asking my mother, "When did I become me? If you had married someone else, would I still have been born? If I was born to different parents, would I still be me, or would I be someone else?" These were questions she couldn't answer, but still, I wanted to know. And so the search began.

I started meditating when I was nineteen, hoping to be enlightened. I followed my teacher's directions carefully: "Sit still and repeat this mantra." He whispered it so lightly into my ear that I wasn't sure I heard it correctly. It was something that resembled, "ieiam." I began repeating it over and over in my mind twice a day, on an empty stomach, for twenty minutes at a time. Breathing in, *I-i-i-i-e-e-e--i*, breathing out, *a-a-a-m-m-m-m*. I was expecting revelation but instead found a swirling mind screaming, *Stop thinking!* Then, *That was a thought.* Followed by, *Stop thinking!* Around and around I'd go: *I'm doing this wrong! AAAUUUUGGGHHH!* And then, *What was that mantra again?*

It had taken years of sitting still before my mind quieted and I tiptoed to the edge of a silent refuge, yet when Lois died, my life-long journey of seeking my true Self was re-stimulated. It was time to return to the underworld for another go 'round the ever-present cycle of personal growth. When facing the loss of my fifty-nine-year-old sister, my outer life paled in comparison to the reality that life would end. One way or another, I realized, *I will draw a final breath.* More than anything, I needed to explore what that meant for me. I dedicated myself to reevaluating how I would spend my remaining life energy. Having awakened to how fast life can pass, I entered into a bearlike hibernation. I needed to untangle mourning the *identity* I'd lost from grieving the *person* I'd lost. I hoped to dream up a new life in the gestating darkness, trusting that, in spring, I would emerge ravenously hungry to feed a fresh start.

Back when I'd known who I was, sitting in the counseling room with clients, I often used the metaphor of a spiral path ascending around a mountain, the peak symbolizing realization of the Self. The same vista—the same wounds, habits, and patterns—is seen again and again, each time from a higher and broader perspective. I under-stood that stumbling in the darkness and falling into rocky crevices was part of the journey—a two-steps-forward-one-step-back kind of trek. With this understanding, I went willingly into the down under. I pulled at threads of memory to unravel the tangled knot of who I'd become, hoping to reweave them into a tapestry of a more authentic me. Nose to the ground, peering through a magnifying glass into my life for a clearer vision on this round of the mountain pass, I con-sciously accepted the journey. Taking my first step into the cave, in which I would begin a major life review, I repeated words my father would shout in the old green Chevy as we rolled over hills and dales, "Hold onto your hat, gals…he-e-e-r-e we go-o-o-o-o!"

Three Sisters

My oldest sister, Sally May Myers, was born on February 14, 1949, then came Lois Joy, several weeks premature, on July 24, 1951, and I—Lynn Susan (I became Lily in 1985, a story for another time)—followed on October 10, 1953. Sally was named for our Great-Uncle Sol and shared a middle name with our mom, Margie May. Lois carried the energy of Daddy Lou, our mom's dad, Louis. I was not named for any ancestor, a rarity in Jewish families.

Like dying, getting born is a big ordeal—a strain on both mother and child, no matter the labor. Our little bodies get squeezed and pressed from all sides, mercilessly pushed out of our warm pool into the tiniest canal, where we swim for our lives. Then we find ourselves thrust into the brightest light, where, greeted by a slap on the butt, our first breath is taken in terror. Whew, welcome to the world, little one! And welcome to your first trauma (of many) in a lifetime. So be it.

I know nothing about Sally's birth, but mine and Lo's were legendary. Being the last in the series, my mom refused all medications and asked that the obstetrician set up mirrors so she could watch my little head arrive into the world. I was what she called a diaphragm baby, coming along earlier than expected and slip-sliding out of the womb with a wild whoosh. I've heard that how a person does anything is how they do everything, and that's pretty much true for me. As my dad once said, "Once you make up your mind to do something, BOOM! Off you go!" He was right; I'm impulsive. I dive headlong into life, holding the optimism torch high. Lois, on the other hand, entered in a huge amount of distress. Back when baby boomers were making their entrances, doctors knew best. Expectant mothers went with the status quo, and since Mom's obstetrician was planning a vacation, they induced labor early. In spite of poor little Lo-ey not being ready, they started the Pitocin drip, and Lois was violently awakened from her quiet pool before her lungs or the rest of her was ready for physical incarnation. She spent the first month of her tiny life in an incubator. Not surprisingly, Lois didn't trust modern medicine. When we went to our family doctor, it was a trial—much crying, coaxing, and red-lollipop rewards ensued. Watching her, I decided I'd be tough and got kudos for taking the shot like a man. I found her intensity of fear inconceivable and sometimes frustrating, but when Lo and I talked about it as adults, we realized that her birth trauma had set her up to view the world through an anxiety lens. Later, when brain cancer stirred layer upon layer of fear for Lois, I felt especially sorry for the little baby who grew up to be a terrified Lo.

The Magothy

Regardless of our unique birth patterns, my family of origin—Sally, Lois, and Lily (the three sisters) and Mason and Margie (the two parents; we called them M&M)—was a solid nuclear family. We were close-knit from early years of summer vacations in the blissful 1950s at the Magothy River, just south of Baltimore. We lived in a log cabin and shared a shower with frogs in the outdoor bathroom. Surrounded by tall pines, the scent of balsam cleaned our insides as we scrubbed away the sandy saltwater of the river each evening. During the day, we crabbed off a splintery wooden pier, tying chicken necks to a string and slowly lowering them into the mud several yards below our dangling feet. Each night we sat on logs overlooking the beach and waited for the multicolored fireworks at the fancy resort across the river. At the end of our two weeks of timeless summer, we celebrated with cousins, grandparents, and extended family, who joined us from their own cabins for a huge crab feast. Tables were spread with Silver Queen corn on the cob, fresh tomatoes, and potato salad. Crabs were steamed in Old Bay seasoning—each giant spidery crustacean a grimy mess. We kids washed 'em clean with a nearby hose. Grown-ups licked their spicy fingertips and cooled their flaming mouths with National Bohemian beer brewed, as commercials reminded us, on the shores of the Chesapeake Bay. It was idyllic. I felt deeply at home, one part of this giant community of people and place. I was crazy about my family.

Our cabin at the Magothy
Uncle Chuck (my dad's brother) crabbing off the pier
Young M&M

The Brick House

We lived in a red brick house with a spacious, covered front porch and a giant backyard. I adored living there, at 2309 Lynhurst Avenue, with red tulips in the front yard and a garden and hammock in the back. That's where I rocked in my Daddy's arms as he lazed and napped on Sunday afternoons. My hero of a dad painted a full-size hopscotch court on the driveway, built a sandbox, and put up a standing swimming pool for summer afternoons. Friends from the neighborhood joined us on the swing set and pushed off on the teeter-totter as we played house in the mini-clapboard Dad put up in the way back. We'd play on the ample front porch after our baths, turning the big white wicker chairs upside down, crawling beneath into our cozy houses. Sometimes we'd spy on "Mr. Asparagus," the strange man next door. Completely oblivious to our giggles, he tended the empty lot and patch of weeds, which I now realize must have been a vegetable garden. On summer nights, Mommy tucked our warm, rosy bodies into bed even before the sun set. Soon Daddy would come home from the store and seal our nighttime ritual with a good-night kiss and rough chin rub. When I heard his car pull into the driveway, I knew he'd soon come sit on the edge of my bed, as he did with all three of us, rubbing his rough beard on my cheek and stroking my hair with a sing-song lullaby, "Nighty night, sleepy pie," until I drifted off. The store was what we called Myers Restaurant, which had grown up from my Pop-Pop's little cigar shop into a full-blown diner.

Myers Restaurant

Pop-Pop arrived at Ellis Island, sailing into the harbor of Lady Liberty as a boy named Zacharia Meyerovitch. He'd come across the salty ocean with my great-grandmother (Bubba—a tough broad I know only by reputation), my great-great grandmother (Lena) and his six siblings. His father, my great-grandfather, seafaring his way around the cape of South Africa ended up fighting in the Boer War and did not join them as planned. They'd been lucky to escape the frightening *pogroms*—a Russian word that describes government-condoned, violent mob attacks against Jews carried out by so-called law-abiding citizens. Devastating to a young Pop-Pop, the pogroms were fraught with random killings, unchecked destruction of homes or businesses, and indiscriminate vandalism. They particularly focused on places of worship, burning the Torah and other holy texts that defined sacred law. Pop-Pop described fear rising in his throat each Sunday, when church bells rang through the village, trumpeting the start of gang violence. Terrified, he and his family prayed to be spared. Escaping the rampant cruelty within their tiny village—Pushalot, Latvia (now Lithuania)—in the late 1800s was their first step toward breathing the air of personal and religious freedom.

Soon Zacharia became Samuel, and Meyerovitch became Myers, his character whitewashed like so many immigrants of the time. Though he outwardly lost a part of his identity, he never lost his inner core—that of a Russian Jew. I can see him now, the ever-present stogie resting in a nearby ashtray or lodged in the corner of his mouth. He often sat in his easy chair, smoke curling up to the ceiling, reading the Yiddish paper cover to cover. Yiddish, a fusion of Eastern European dialects spoken across cultures, was a unifying force among persecuted peoples. It was a part of his soul; something I only heard him share at home with my grandma. Neither the Cossacks nor the Nazis could take that language away, and it kept his identity intact. Its remnants weave through my own life, reminding me of the history of my lineage, the proud ethnicity from which I am born.

When he was still a boy, Bubba pulled Sam and his favorite brother, my Great-Uncle Sol, from school. As young teens, they had to help support the family. For something like five cents a week, they worked in a cigar factory. Sweeping up the dropped tobacco from the floor, Sam also swept up knowledge. Eventually, by the time they were sixteen, he and Sol graduated to cigar rolling. He never made it back to school, but Pop-Pop prided himself on becoming educated, though his Latvian accent, exacerbated by the cigar clenched between his teeth, gave away his status as an immigrant. (I was an adult before I learned that the "Benzo" clock, which he wound religiously with a key and which chimed consistently on the hour, was really a banjo clock.) Young Sam went to night classes and read voraciously while he and Sol learned the ropes of the whole cigar shindig: importing Cuban tobacco, how to roll a good one, knowing the difference between a quality smoke and a cheap one. I don't think I ever saw my grandfather without a cigar, the aromatic scent of the smoke mixed with the warm feeling of a tough hug, a rough kiss, and a pinched cheek or collar.

Pop-Pop and Uncle Sol on the corner of Charles and Redwood
Pop-Pop and Dad on the same corner decades later

One day, as two young men with a vision, Pop-Pop and Uncle Sol left the factory and opened their own small store on the corner of Charles and Redwood Streets in downtown Baltimore. Sam and Sol took great pride in sitting in the window of the shop, rolling cigars. Soon they had a successful business of their own, becoming respected men in their community. But it was during Prohibition that Grandma Lil helped to expand the store. With bars and pubs in the neighborhood closed, she made sandwiches that sold like crazy. When my father, the firstborn son, joined the family business after World War II, he took things further, adding a sandwich counter to the smoky cigar shop. This became Myers Restaurant, featuring a red-and-white tile floor beneath Formica tables and booths. Waitresses wearing little aprons and mesh caps served hot turkey sandwiches—Wonder Bread beneath the meat, smothered in gravy. The scent transports me to a red vinyl booth with just one whiff every time. Cigars, of course, always held an esteemed place in the humidors behind the clunky cash register.

Pop-Pop once took us to see the Broadway musical *Fiddler on the Roof,* where he sat between four granddaughters just a few rows behind the orchestra pit. Weeping, he watched the story of his life—persecution woven with loss—acted out upon the stage. The musical ended with Jewish villagers packing up their belongings and trudging off in search of freedom while the solitary fiddler played his melancholy violin. The melody pierced my heart as I watched the lone man perched precariously on the roof, the narrator reminding us that freedom is as tentative "as a...as a...as a fiddler on the roof!" The music of the grand finale swelled, and we cried along with Pop-Pop, tears falling onto our fancy dresses. We'd awakened to the persecution from whence we came—our ancestral wound and our brave heritage. My father, my father's father, and his father, too, carry wounds of abandonment, victimization, and isolation. We also carry the courage to seek a more whole existence. I feel a responsibility, as if I am carrying these qualities and wounds for them—as if I am on a healing quest, not only for myself but also in service to those who have come before me. I am now, as I was then, deeply connected to my grandfather's story. It has always been so, this patriarchal lineage residing at the core of my identity. After all, it was my name, too, that had been stripped away. I know myself as a Myers. But really, truly, in my most indigenous self, I am a Meyerovitch.

The Meyerovitch Clan
Bubba
My ancestral altar

The Heritage House

In 1960, the year I turned seven, the City of Baltimore entered a period of redevelopment, and Myers Restaurant was displaced. Nothing new to us; we packed up our belongings, as Jews have done since the exodus from Egypt, and moved on. This time it was not from the brutality of a persecuting pogrom but as a deeply ingrained migratory pattern that continued down the Myers line. It was exciting as Myers Restaurant relocated from downtown Baltimore to Howard County, adopting a brand-new identity: *The Heritage House*. The stone building was massive (I thought it was a castle) and stood on the corner of St. John's Lane and Route 40 in tiny Ellicott City. Surrounded by expansive lawns, with a motel behind and a huge parking lot in front, the castle sat at the edge of a highway that featured a blinking yellow light and a lonely Greyhound bus stop.

We left the red brick house to live upstairs from the restaurant. Two apartments became one long string of rooms after a wall was turned into a doorway. "Out the road" is what Pop-Pop and Dad called it since it was way out in the country, surrounded by pastures and cornfields. I fed grass to lambs at the school-bus stop and watched a calf being born in a field. My dad changed the name to reflect his warm and welcoming spirit, calling it *Mason's Heritage House and Ye Olde English Pub*. He added "Come as you are..." in red letters on the enormous black and white sign visible from my bedroom window or Lo's, where the warm glow of a neon sign advertising "Cocktails" in cursive pink letters reflected off the window glass.

Though we didn't know it yet, this exciting move was when we lost our father to his dream. Gone were lazy sun-drenched Sunday's in the hammock or trips to the zoo where we fed peanuts to monkeys and watched lions and bears, Dad's favorites. Gone were big white-wicker chairs where, fresh from our baths, Lois and I played in the safety zone of home and hearth. Gone were the comforts of Dad's sandpapery five-o'clock shadow on soft five-year-old skin as I was tucked in for the night. The sweet rituals were replaced by phone calls downstairs for virtual good-night kisses. I curled fetal-like, feet tight under me, scared something might chew my little toes in the night but bravely tucking my own self into bed. Instead of a front door atop brick steps to a generous porch, the entrance to our apartment was a long, dark stairway from a heavy but unlocked wooden door where restaurant deliveries were made (and maybe scary men could slip into my bedroom with a knife!). With no parents sitting in the living room once we kids were in bed, I'd decide each night whether to turn my back to the wall for protection or to hide my face in sleepy denial. "Nighty night, sleepie pie..." was replaced by a nightly mantra I'd sing-song to myself, tough bravado meeting lonely fears in bed. I chanted to myself, "*Fair-ies...can-dies...twinkle-twinkle-little-star...sweet stuff... fair-ies...cotton can-dy...Tinkerbell...*" These words soothed me into safety and sleep. My parents were immersed in their new business, building a livelihood, and I entered second grade at a new school.

We ate all our meals in the restaurant, ordering off the menu. It was glamorous being waited upon as we nibbled dill pickles from the monkey dish set carefully between tall glowing candles. It later became tiresome, when I longed for real family dinners around our homemade table. Mom and Dad ate separately, after the dinner rush, but Mom sat at the table with us as we ate. Dad, like a jumping jack, came and went, punctuating our stories by popping up to greet guests or fix the temperamental dishwasher. To the staff and patrons, I'm sure it appeared that we were a happy family—and we were—but without thinking, as if by osmosis, I learned to hold my stories inside. It was less painful to hold my treasures back than to be cut off mid-story, put aside for a stranger or a mechanical being. As the youngest, it was easy to sit back and watch my older and more facile sisters regale with tales. Sally got us laughing with the shenanigans of teenage boys from her class while Lois outlined her latest science project. No one noticed that I had become quiet or knew that I rarely did my homework. I simply said, "Done!" The small lie covered an aloneness that I hid even from myself.

The Heritage House
Menu from Myers Restaurant
Heritage House Logo
Myers Restaurant (Uncle Sol to left of counter/Pop-Pop to the right)

The Temple of Milrace

Any time Dad needed us, he'd come to the bottom of the stairs and whistle. Like obedient dogs, we'd run to see what he wanted, careful not to step loudly and disturb the patrons beneath our floors. Sometimes, on a balmy Sunday night when business was slow, Dad would whistle, and Sal, Lo, and I would take a quick look at each other before exclaiming, "Crabs!" We knew that Sunday-evening whistle! It was a signal to put on an old shirt because we'd be heading out to messy Milrace Tavern. Milrace was nestled at the bottom of a curved street, a small cul-de-sac bordered by a tangle of honeysuckle on one side and a wide, muddy creek on the other. The humid night blanketed our bare arms, the sweet smell of summer surrounding us as we gathered for the holiest of Myers ceremonies, the Maryland Crab Ritual. Inside, we were greeted like family, the smells of vinegar and stale beer mingling with Old Bay's heavy dose of garlic and pepper. The slight under scent of mildew from the creek settled on the worn wooden dance floor. It was the smell of deep familiarity and communal solidarity. Grinning in anticipation and licking our lips, we entered into the temple of Milrace and gathered around the wood-plank tables covered in newspaper. Like Marylanders everywhere, we salivated in preparation for the burning sensation to come. Families or couples at nearby tables enacted the same ritual, leaning over to share a joke, tossing aside proper manners, spitting crab shells onto the table, competing to see who could make the biggest pile. No one worried about a wink from a stranger; we were all one big crab-eatin' family!

Charlie (pronounced Chaa-lie) was always there, playing jazz piano with one hand and a bluesy organ with the other. The music, big-band era, was full and rich, a backdrop to boiling-hot spice-laden steamed crabs dished out alongside a dance floor worn smooth from cha-chas and two-steps. Margie and Mace enjoyed a beer or two and we girls, Coca-Cola. Most importantly, we got to stay up late dancing. I loved the gritty romance of those Sunday nights: hands plunged into the messy crabs balanced with smooth moves on the dance floor. Laughing, singing along with Chaa-lie's tunes, running free, and making a big mess was an earthy heaven—a cornucopia of pleasures of body and soul. A stop at Howard Johnson's for ice-cream cones, the one place open twenty-four hours a day in the early 1960s, was part of the tradition—a sweet harmony to the salty crabs. We completed the ceremony at home by squeezing lemon juice over our hands to cleanse the fishy smell of crab from our fingers.

Ye Olde English Pub

Home—twenty steps up from the restaurant, to be exact—was where Dad took afternoon naps on the red couch to keep pace with serving three meals a day and a pub open until two in the morning. He'd been a star fencer at Johns Hopkins University, and his swords graced the dark paneled walls of Ye Olde English Pub, hanging among shields he'd cut from plywood and painted with stripes and symbols. His idealistic fantasy—being a knight of the round table—surrounded him. That was our dad, standing for the good, the right, and the mighty. He painted a red lion-dragon seal on the back of a round sled, the symbol of his Leo-the-Lion soul, centered between crossed fencing swords from his days at Hopkins. Dad was in his prime and living his purpose. He was also very busy proving himself a successful businessman to his demanding father.

Pop-Pop—the self-made man that he was—had high expectations. He loved hard, but his early life of suffering and persecution—combined with his demanding, tough broad of a mother—made him a man who judged harshly and expected perfection. Winning Sam's approval drove Mason, like any good Jewish firstborn son, to work at full speed and at all costs, never realizing the expense it exacted from his own daughters. Like father like son—my dad was a staunch perfectionist. He went beyond correcting our grammar—he often quizzed us on the present-participle-subjugated-verb-object-pronoun thing. If I said "I" in a sentence and he said "Who?" I realized that I should've said "Me." We're not "eatin' supper," as Sally once said to a friend on the phone, we're "having dinner." Being on time meant being fifteen minutes early, but in case we got a flat on the way, we'd better leave extra time, which meant we were, embarrassingly, always half an hour early. His impatient adage, "Stop your bellyachin' or I'll give you somethin' to cry about!" taught us to be cautious and careful, often hiding out in our rooms. Tucked in toes aside, I learned to suck it up and "stop acting like a baby." Parents are supposed to guide their children into putting their best foot forward, but with my dad, it was like putting two best feet out in front. I couldn't find any place to stand, for fear of making a mess.

Living right upstairs, our lives revolved around the restaurant. Because my parents kept Ye Olde English Pub open until the two-o'clock last call, they slept late each morning. At seven years old, I was expected to behave responsibly, which meant getting up in time to make breakfast and a sack lunch (or order it from the restaurant), make my bed, be sure that the newspaper was placed quietly at the foot of Mom and Dad's bed, and catch the school bus. It went without saying that my homework was done and neatly inserted into my book bag. But meeting these demands was nothing compared to the sudden explosion of anger that would rain down if we drank the last bit of milk without refilling the bottle from the downstairs milk machine. My dad could be devilishly scary—stomping around the room, hands animated, finger jabbing at the air as he shouted about how hard he worked to put a roof over our heads. Why weren't we more grateful for all he was doing for us? Like a three-year-old in a tantrum, he had amnesia, forgetting that he was fulfilling his own dream. Minimizing my impact on him became an art.

When Dad wasn't unexpectedly erupting in a volcanic tantrum, he was dedicated, sometimes bordering on stoic. Since Pop-Pop had to sacrifice his home and his education to survive, he'd passed down stoicism born of persecution. It was a habit that masked the pain of abandonment. My dad worked hard to prove himself worthy to his father, and I did the same with him. We all wanted to please Dad—his love meant everything. As we entered our teen years, we each worked at the restaurant—Lois and Sally worked the front of the house as waitresses while I remained in the kitchen. I was tucked into a cubby in the salad room, where I sat in front of an ancient cash register, singing out a loud "cha-ching" each time I rang up a meal. At the end of the night, tallying the checks and counting the cash with my dad was a matter of great pride. I held my breath while he added up the coins and bills, then calculated the expected total. It wouldn't take long to find out whether the checks and balances came out even. Close wasn't good enough; I expected perfection to the penny. That was how I earned his respect, a respect that felt an awful lot like love.

Ad-ventcha!

Eventually, economic development ousted the business so that The Heritage House and the Myers clan migrated back into the city. The times, they were a changin'—it was the summer of love—and Ye Olde English Pub morphed into the Zodiac Lounge. Mason's Heritage House was on the first floor of a brand-new high-rise office building. With construction underway, we took to the road, eating our way into oblivion in the name of restaurant research. It was a grand adventure (we pronounced it "ad-ventcha!"). We cruised through the USA in our Chevrolet, gathering ideas for the new restaurant. We discovered salad bars and avocados. We ate at a Greek restaurant in San Francisco, where we had our first taste of souvlaki as Lois flirted with the handsome olive-skinned waiter. Waving napkins in the air, like Zorba the Greek, we line danced around the table at the end of our meal. For six weeks, we crammed ourselves and a cooler into our brand-new, silver-blue Impala. Carting hooded hair dryer and curlers, shorts and sun-dresses, cowboy hats and fringed moccasins, we meandered through the Wild West, down the Pacific Coast, and into the vastness of the Grand Canyon. On that trip, somewhat to the embarrassment of his three hippie teens, our dad, a cowboy at heart, grew a beard and wore a Stetson. He bought one for Mom, too. She only tossed it aside during her infamous "bug dance" at Jenny Lake. Out of nowhere, she'd shrieked, jumped three feet off her rock, and started ripping off her clothes, shouting and twirling. Apparently a spider, or something worse, crawled inside her jump-suit and took a bite of her belly. The four of us laughed hysterically, completely incapable of helping her. She, too, chuckled through her screams, tears of laughter streaming down her cheeks—a signature Margie moment. As a family, we kept a journal of our journey, and in it we recorded the event as "a happening!"

More than a demanding father, Dad was the hero in his own story, and he was our hero, too. Each morning, he'd throw open the motel-room curtains and shout, "Everybody up! Shake a leg! The sun is over the pumpkin!" He liked to say that he was the light-bulb around which his four girls flitted, like moths drawn to the flame. He was the lionhearted king of our family, a bright sun, and we followed his lead in all things. It wasn't until much later that I questioned this imagery, realizing the dangerous nature of being the moth.

Mourning as My Path

Though these stories made me into me, I long ago entered therapy and discovered I was more than a moth drawn to the flame. Yet after losing three-fifths of my birth family, I revisited the blessings and curses of my childhood, especially as I mourned Lois and relived much of her cancer journey. Grieving flooded me with memories. As they floated to the surface, I untangled the knotted threads of being loved and cared for *and* abandoned and neglected. Both were equally true (there was no blaming involved). I embraced the blessings and curses of my good-enough childhood as two sides to one coin. Becoming independent at an early age enabled me to take risks I might never otherwise have hazarded—a blessing. Being neglected engendered a pattern of self-neglect—a curse. I'd learned to be fiercely independent, to face my fears and overcome them, and to believe in my dreams. I'd absorbed the habit of righteously sacrificing my emotional needs for the greater good, as if it were the right way to be and as if being unattended was the norm. Abandonment—a deeply personal core wound, and an ancestral one—inspired me to become strong and independent, but it also caused deep loneliness and isolation. I visited the same vistas I'd seen before, circling around the mountain where new vantage points showed me the blessings and curses as part and parcel of the same thing. One does not exist without the other: light and dark, happy and sad, strong and vulnerable, wounded and perpetrator.

As I mourned, I discovered how deeply identified I was with my father's lineage, while knowing almost nothing about my mother's. I also began to realize that, although my personality was formed by these paradoxes, I was so much more than my personality. Grief became like an archaeological dig on the path to my spirit. Reviewing and examining my life revealed layer after layer of sedimentary strata, personality traits covering my most innate ground of being—my Self.

Two

Being Human

We played hard; we fought hard. I was the boss because I was older, and she let me do it, though she really didn't have much of a choice. She was the one who idolized me, and I, with a child's mind, sat on the pedestal. And I loved her very much.

When Lily was six and I nine, we lost our parents to the restaurant above which we lived. Our bond became tighter and much more intense, as we suddenly had to take more responsibility for ourselves.

—Lois

The Paradox of Me and Lo

I kept digging. Hanging on the proverbial hook, I pondered the paradox of me: capable and needy, community builder and isolated, lost and found. Revisiting my memories of Lois, I soon discovered that the story of me and Lo was also paradoxical. We were symbiotic with one another—like an infinity symbol, with no beginning or end—weaving a tale of love and hurt. Lois and I played joyfully in our shared bedroom in the red brick house, tossing our stuffed animals back and forth in the dark for good-night kisses before drifting to sleep, a favorite toy wrapped in our arms. Though we sometimes drew invisible lines to command our own space, we also made it beautiful together. We'd pile every-thing—a huge mound of trinkets, toys, dresses, and shoes—into the center of the room and then, one by one, assess what to keep or toss, placing our most treasured knickknacks carefully aside. We were partners in the truest sense, thinking and acting as one to create our agreed-upon view of beauty. Every renovation ended with our matching musical jewelry boxes placed just so upon identical multicolored dressers, each box surrounded by a finely tuned display of exotic dolls our grandmother had brought from her foreign travels: the perfect tableau. Once, when Mom gave us permission to gleefully jump on our beds for five minutes, I fell onto the sharp corner of Lois's desk drawer, splitting a gash in my skull. I screamed so loudly the neighbors looked up from their dinners; Lois, on the other side of the room, screamed, too. Many years later, she told me that she'd cried because she felt my pain, not for fear of getting in trouble, as everyone had assumed.

But that space is also where we fought—stridently and often. If Sally heard us yelling argumentatively and stepped in to mediate, we'd simultaneously turn (connected even in conflict) and, without a signal, blast our rage onto Sal with a shared, "Leave us alone!" Yet when I cut her Ginny doll's hair (truly thinking it would grow back, just like mine) or smeared greasy Vaseline over the entire dresser (so shiny!), I was in BIG trouble. Worse than any punishment from Mom was tolerating the excruciatingly long wait for Lois's anger to dissipate, when she would play with me again. When I asked my mom for a pocketbook and she bought it for me, Lois railed, "You never bought *me* a pocketbook!" Too young to be aware of money issues, I had simply asked, while Lois, sensitive to their concerns, had held back.

She was my Big Sister and I her canvas. When we played beauty parlor, she insisted on the role of creative designer, and I would always comply. Turning my unruly bangs into a "spring curl," which bounced back into shape when squeezed, was her favorite design. I hated that curl but loved her fawning. Though I begged her to switch roles, it was never allowed. I suppose she was also under the spell of our critical father, acting out his perfectionist power issues in her own way, because touching Lois's long, wavy locks was taboo, as was sitting on her bed lest I make it shake. I agreed to her rules just to get her attention or win her approval. I idolized her. Playing with her gave me a big, expansive feeling in my chest, and I felt lucky when she shined her light on me.

When we lived out the road, our games matched the wider world of field and forest. Lo and I knew it was silly when we tied a string around Daffy's neck. He was Sally's pet duck, but it was Lo and I who waddled him across the grassy, dandelion-dotted meadow to wade in the bubbling stream in the back beyond. Fearing he would swim downstream, we took turns holding tight to our end of the long string. When Dad decided that Daffy'd outgrown his cage, we all agreed to release him into the big lake at Druid Hill Park. Hearing his nervous, high-pitched quack-quacking as the deeper-voiced quackers gathered round for inspection broke our little hearts. Lo cried, but I didn't—*I* was all grown up.

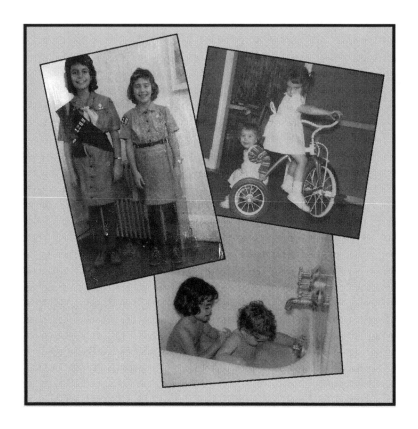

My Big Sister and me

Lois's softhearted love for birds had begun long before that day. She was nine and I seven when I helped her choose Peppy from the cages at the back of McCrory's five-and-dime. He was, by all accounts, *her* bright-green parakeet, but together we learned how to give him seeds and water without his escaping or pecking our hands. We'd close my bedroom door, open his cage, and he'd fly free, landing on our shoulders or outstretched fingers as we laughed and he screeched. We tried to teach him to say, "Hello," by repeating it over and over, with zero success, and we each devotedly took turns cleaning his cage until one morning when we found him on its floor, having died in the night.

In winter, we bundled up to play in the snow, with layers of long johns, flannel-lined blue jeans, snow pants, and red rubber boots pulled over three pairs of socks and lace-up oxfords. Abominable snow-women, we trudged into the fluff and agreed which pristine fields would remain untouched, reserved for the oh-so-important act of gazing at freshly fallen snow. Plus, we vowed, they were reserved ONLY for making snow angels. We held these agreements as sacred, thinking as one, believing in beauty. Clambering through snow-laden pine branches to rock outcroppings, we'd see who could find the longest icicle for a magic wand, until noses and toes were frozen and we'd head inside to peel off each wet layer, standing over newspapers on the kitchen linoleum. Once boots were lined up and clothes carefully laid on toasty iron radiators, we'd brew a pot of warm milk for cocoa, which we sipped as our toes slowly defrosted. Heaven.

Sally was Lois's Big Sister, but for me, Sally was unreachable, the one whose directives I had to obey—the babysitter, not the playmate. In any given moment, Lois might stop in the middle of a game to talk about boys with Sally. Abandoned and left out of their grown-up games, the expanse in my chest would shrink. I learned to hold my enthusiasm back, never knowing when I would become the less-than sister, the odd girl out. It was subtle, this feeling that I didn't measure up, but it became second nature to play second fiddle. Without fanfare, I took a backseat, watching carefully from the sidelines for what would win approval. I acted all big and independent, but I felt tiny inside, hiding my belief that I could never catch up with my sisters. I adopted the expectation that this was how it would always be. Without realizing it, I'd stopped knowing how to belong and started trying to figure out who *to* become, with hopes of just fitting in instead.

As pubescent teens, Lois became both my closest ally and my biggest critic. When she found me lying on the daybed one afternoon, abandoning myself to a bag of divinely crunchy cheese curls, her words, "You're disgusting!" embedded themselves deep into my psyche. I rebelled by digging even deeper into that bag of orange, cheesy messiness, comforting myself with carbs. Beyond the sensational taste, serotonin calmed my anxieties. Pleasure offered comfort for cruel words and my increasing loneliness.

Finally Lo went to a different school, and I began to flourish in mine. From becoming yearbook editor to founding a student foreign-exchange program to making it onto the peppy cheerleader squad, I found myself among the popular crowd. Still, I sought Lo's guidance in everything from makeup (as natural gals, we preferred Vaseline to Maybelline mascara and Noxzema to CoverGirl) to boys (love me for my mind, not my body!) to how to dress (don't wear the same thing two days in a row—duh!).

The paradox of Lois—the idolized and beautiful sister transposed against the harsh and hurtful one—was confusing. The marriage of connection and rejection settled under the surface of who I became in the world, living in the downstairs of my psyche. I was not conscious of the boiling cauldron brewing up a perfect stew of hurt and hope. Mixed messages formed my mixed up identity; I truly did not know who I was, only who I wanted to be to win her—or anyone's—approval.

Love and Betrayal

When Lo headed to college, the tension between us miraculously evaporated. It melted away so completely that I enjoyed sleepover weekends with her at the University of Maryland. In my hippie costume of the day—torn and patched jeans topped with a baggy flannel shirt—I followed her lead, trying beer, wine, pot, and sitting in candlelit rooms with sitar music in the background. She majored in arts and crafts, and I often helped her work on a project, invariably at the final hour. I didn't see myself as an artist—that was Lo's role—but I was her cheerleader, thinking that everything she made was extraordinary. Because it was.

By the time Lo came home from college and moved back in with M&M, I'd been living with Corry for over a year. Seven years my senior, he was the first man who asked me what I thought about life and how I felt about mine in particular. I'd pretty much stopped having an opinion at ten when Dad admonished me with, "Get to the point already!" as I babbled my way through a story for which he had no patience. Once, when asked what I thought of a movie, I hedged, thankful when someone else piped up so that I could figure out what to think. I answered only when I knew the right answer. When Corry asked me what I really cared about, sitting in an overgrown cemetery behind my house, my vague answer was, "Um... plants...maybe nature." I got more excited as I told him about a book I'd been reading, which said that talking to plants helped them grow. The idea that plants and humans had a real connection—an energetic relationship—captured my imagination. With his urging, I found a job in a greenhouse, falling completely in love with sinking my hands into soil and growing aromatic carnations and colorful mums—flowers to be cut for the attached flower shop. Watering geraniums, petunias, and poinsettias became a daily ritual in which the plants and I had long conversations as I nurtured them from seedling to bloom. Corry re-fathered me; he listened as I struggled to find my own voice. But, like my father, he had strong opinions. He shaped me into the kind of woman he wanted me to become, and I wanted to be her, whoever she was. He taught me to change the oil in my 1963 dark-green Volvo, how to clean and tap the spark plugs for optimum firing, and how to reset the timing on the car's distributor. He showed me how to be tough in the daytime and soft in the night.

We sat on the front-porch steps at the end of each day, Corry covered in sawdust from woodworking and I with chlorophyll-tinged fingers and dirt under my nails. Our two dogs, Tanya and Molly, sprawled behind us or chased groundhogs in the deepening dusk. Corry would lean against the faded porch post, scratching his beard, taking a swig of beer, and sighing with contentment as I rested against his knees. We'd watch the dogs tumble together—teeth to neck, tongues hanging loose as they rollicked—until the air finally cooled and the sky painted itself in subtle pastel watercolors. Slowly, fireflies lighted their lanterns, and the dogs returned and climbed into our waiting laps. Their kisses filled me with the scent of freedom—a taste of life as it should be: tired body, fulfilled hearts, and deep breaths.

This was the era of free love, the early 1970s, when everyone was playing around with sexual orientation, threesomes, collective marriages, drugs, and rock and roll. Corry and I had an open relationship, which meant that, though we lived together and shared a bank account, dating and sleeping with others was allowed. I'd agreed to this because I wanted to be with him, not because I wanted it. After more than a year of living together, without any outside dating, my fingers were crossed that it would never happen.

Lois became an integral part of this life. I continued to idolize her, but bickering was a thing of the past; beyond being sisters, we were friends. When she asked me to help her at an art fair up in State College, Pennsylvania, I jumped at the chance. After the long drive through the mountains, I unfolded myself from my green Volvo and wandered through aisle after aisle of amazing arts and crafts. Searching for Lo's booth, I was intimidated by the exotic world of Creative People. Everything was high quality handmade, and everyone was an Artist but me. I shrank into shyness, becoming an onlooker, a mere mortal who could barely muster the courage to ask directions, much less have a conversation. But as the days wore on, because I was with my hip, beautiful, and exotic sister, I got a pass, an entrée into that world of Creatives. We went to someone's house for a potluck and ended up staying the night, spreading our sleeping bags among others crashed on the living-room floor. I could hardly believe it! *I'm just hangin' with the Artists!* I tried to be cool, wishing I could be one of them.

I got that chance when we returned home and Lo turned down a teaching gig as an arts-and-crafts teacher at Baltimore County Adult Education, passing it on to me. I was stunned that she thought I could do it, having absolutely no clue about my own creativity. Lois became *my* cheerleader, convincing me that "being an artist isn't about being able to paint or draw, and it isn't what you make; it's about how you live. Your *life* is your art," she said. "You are an artist!"

Incredulous and scared, I let her convince me, accepted the job, and proved her right. I led the class of mostly women in everything from arranging fresh flowers (I hauled bucketful's of seconds from my job at the greenhouse) to collecting, drying, and arranging wildflowers. I taught the needlework and embroidery skills I'd inherited from my maternal grandmother, Mommy Helen. But mostly what happened in that class was that I discovered my natural instinct for teaching. I found that, beyond instruction on specific crafts, I was able to engage the group in the most extraordinary conversations about life, values, and spiritual beliefs. As needles moved in and out of fabric and the aroma of chrysanthemums wafted through our chatter, we came to know one another—and ourselves—as creative souls. And that is how I discovered that, like Lois, I was an artist, too. It was in me all along.

I'd found an identity. I'd become the woman Corry wanted, the artist Lois believed in, and the Greenhouse Grower who loved her work. I loved the image of the woman I thought I was, having fallen softly into a niche of becoming. At twenty I was starting to believe in my own worth, joyfully changing into colorful peasant skirts with hiking boots beneath and a Swiss Army Knife in my sewn-in pocket once I'd scrubbed my nails clean at the end of each day. I still changed the oil, now in my turquoise Datsun pickup, and I felt alive and happy with the image of self I'd begun to discover.

One summer evening, I stopped at Corry's shop on my way home, where he was building a camper for the Datsun. We'd designed it together for a soon-to-be cross-country camping dream. Corry's woodworking shop, in a barely renovated chicken coop, was next door to Lo's pottery studio. Always proud to call Lois a member of my blood family, I treasured how organically she blended with my created family. As Corry and I sat in the evening glow of a pinking sky and passed a bottle of beer between us, he turned, looked me deep in the eyes, and in the most casual way, said, "I think I'm falling in love with your sister." My world stopped cold; all thought and emotion came to a screeching halt. I was dumbstruck. Literally, I could not speak. White noise filled my head. As if in slow motion I stood, left the beer in the grass, and with a mouth as dry as bone and legs somehow walking, I moved toward my turquoise truck. I could barely hear Corry, a distant voice calling my name, yelling something like, "Wait! Let's talk about this!" I couldn't look at him, much less respond to his calls. All I could think was, *Of course you're in love with her. Everyone is.*

I'd agreed to an open relationship, to dating others, but my sister? She was the one I could never keep up with. I could never be as beautiful, as sexy, or (let's face it) as skinny as Lois. My sister, with whom I was just beginning to feel that *maybe* we could be equal. And he wasn't talking about dating or having sex with her; he was falling in love with her. I knew I'd lost. Without knowing *what* I'd lost, I simply knew that I had. Somehow, somewhere deep inside, I'd become less than once again, knowing I would never, ever win. With Corry's words, my core belief was reconfirmed. I did not belong.

I have absolutely no recollection of what happened next, whether I went home or for a drive, or what happened when Corry came home that night. I don't remember a conversation

with him, though I'm sure we had one. I only remember that
Lois came to me several days later and asked how I'd feel if she
slept with Corry. He'd approached her about wanting to make
love, and she wanted to do it, but "only if you feel OK about it."
As offhanded as he'd been, she followed with, "Really, I'm completely fine either way." I heard her asking permission through a
deep fog. I had no idea what to feel, and with no one to turn to
for guidance, the image of who I thought I'd become was shattered. Saying no to Lois—who had been my idol, my mentor, and
my cheerleader for creativity—was impossible. Images of spring
curls and phrases like, "You're disgusting," blended with those
of pristine snow angels and dolls lined up in a perfect tableau.
Sadly, I put on a face of bravado and with a shrug, said, "Sure,
no sweat." It was a not-so-small lie to cover a big feeling: I was
deeply inadequate. Mixed signals prevailed. Lois, my avid cheerleader, and Lois, my aggravating critic—love and rejection. Lois,
my idol, and Lois, my abandoner—better than and less than.
Lois, my blood, and Lois, my betrayer—connection and pain.
Those were the two sides to the coin of Lois and me, the eternal
paradox. I gave permission where none should ever have been
granted. Lois had asked for something she wanted, like I'd asked
for a pocketbook, and like my mother, I gave it.

We were part of a changing world where being free sexually and
otherwise was valued. This is what I told myself, burying the hatchet
so deep that it would be decades before the sharp blade of truth would
rise up and cut us apart. But with all that as yet unknown, Corry and I
packed our camper and set out, meeting up with Lo at a craft fair and
sleeping in tents among Artists, where I lay rigid in my lone sleeping

bag, my head buried and ears covered to muffle the sounds of my mate coupling with my sister. Late in the night, I emerged from beneath my pillow to listen to the silent forest pierced only by the clashing swords of an inner battle between low self-esteem and self-preservation. My emotions flared as I came to the realization that this could never—must never, *ever* happen again. The next day, bouncing on the hard bench seat of the Datsun, a different kind of silence, so loud it was palpable, filled the truck. Breathing heavily, I told him, "I don't want you to sleep with Lois again." I'd found my limit, my voice. In spite of, or perhaps because of, the night before, I was growing in courage and strength. Corry simply said, "OK," but none of us could see how long that night would simmer beneath the surface of me.

That was the beginning of the end for Corry and me. It culminated one night, a month later, when I threw a feather pillow at his head as hard as I could and then screamed, "I hate you!" at his retreating back. The words cut through the thick night air, and later, sitting inside our camper, I realized that to really find myself, beyond any image, I needed to be alone. I drove off in the truck, leaving Corry, thumb extended, to hitch his way through the West. That's when I started the long, slow journey of learning, at last, how to re-father myself.

Moving on to Hawk Mountain

Relieved and freed from my relationship with Corry, my tensions about Lois dissipated. I told myself that he was to blame, not her. Fears that he would love her more became irrelevant. She and I just moved on, preserving our connection through a complicit silence. We entered new relationships; I moved through some sweet and troubled ones, choosing the same kind of man over and over—one who could not cherish me as I longed to be cherished. I fell in love with wounded, absent men like my father. In spite of newfound self-fathering, I was still a girl seeking her father's love and respect, so each man played out some quality of my actual father. I read someplace that we parent ourselves in the same way we were parented. That means that no matter how we're wounded—and I don't think anyone escapes being wounded, no matter how much we are loved—we'll somehow recapitulate it in an attempt, as adults, to heal it. Choosing men like my father, over and over, was more than unsatisfying. It was painful.

Lois had relationship struggles of her own when she hooked up with David L., who Sally and I call Dave-One. An outdoorsman, he wooed Lo with his ability to swing from tree branches like a monkey and to name flora and stalk fauna in the wild woods behind the Artist's commune where he lived. She did not realize that his good looks, buff body, and macho countenance masked a needy tendency toward tantrums when he felt threatened. Lois's inclination as a social butterfly pushed his needy button long and often.

In spite of his issues, she loved him. He introduced us to a new world when he invited us to a predawn trek to Hawk Mountain for an annual bird count. Waking way before the crack of dawn and loaded down with thermoses, coolers, blankets, and binoculars, we stuffed ourselves into the car, drove into southern Pennsylvania and then hiked to the lookout. We settled in the chill autumn air among boulders and fellow bird-watchers. Lo and I shared Dad's huge old binocs from the 1950s—they must have weighed a bazillion pounds—and waited for birds of prey to pass us by. We learned that they caught updrafts of breezes caused by warming cliffs along their migratory route. The other folks there, more experienced with the ins and outs of bird-watching, showed us how to keep a lookout for a speck in the sky, then train our binoculars on it to track its flight. Lois and I shared the exhilaration of a bald eagle flying straight at us, its white feathers and yellow beak trained full-on toward our first-time eagle-viewing faces, our hearts beating wildly. We could see the eyes of this majestic bird through the lens of the hefty binoculars as it effortlessly glided directly at us. Lo and I passed the lenses back and forth, sharing that memorable moment. I imagine it as the exact second she fell in love with bird-watching.

Relationship Mirrors

Lois and Dave-One soon packed up their belongings and migrated toward warmer weather. They settled in dusty Austin, Texas—the musical home of Willie Nelson and Lyle Lovett—long before the high-tech boom brought thousands of jobs and out-of-control development. Lo had fancied herself a cowgirl since she had been a tot with a ten-gallon hat flopping down over her eyes. The red-and-white fringed cowgirl skirt and vest, complete with cowboy boots and gun holster, had been her favorite outfit. In junior high, she learned all the songs to *Annie Get Your Gun* and dressed as Annie Oakley one Halloween. The cowboy capital and liberal enclave of Austin, with its strong environmental movement and eccentric, artsy vibe, was a place in which she felt right at home.

A few years later, in 1980, I also migrated south to Austin, where I camped out on Lo and Dave-One's living-room floor until I found a place of my own. Lo had just bought a kiln and parked it in the carport, mixing glazes and trying new designs. I witnessed the first ceremonial unloading of the kiln on the night before Lo's Austin debut, when she found out, the hard way, that an electric kiln was a whole new ball game. The clay had bubbled where it should have been smooth and standby glazes turned pockmarked on pots of yucky green and yuckier yellow, leaving a stunned Lois collapsing into exhausted sobs. Her tears escalated the ever-present tension in her home with Dave. He had no idea how to handle Lo's anxiety. When she pushed herself to the brink of exhaustion, completing a project at the final hour, she needed empathy, but his, "Well, you shouldn't have waited so long!" undermined her confidence even more than the failed firing. Even when no crisis loomed, Dave was a winner at sulking. If Lo was rushing off to soccer instead of cooking at the stove like Grandma, pans got to clanging and cabinets banging. She just cringed, then hid like a battered wife from girlfriends. But she often appeared at my doorstep, where, safe in my arms, she cried, ranted, and complained. Each time they reached a boiling point and she came close to leaving, a hike or camping trip would make things better. For a while. She made friends with that kiln, though, and her pottery flourished as her relationship floundered. She coaxed it into giving her warm browns and neutrals, which gave way to her blue period and finally to the spotted beige glaze with exquisite carvings. Lois took risks with her art, experimenting with indigenous methods of pit firing, and won a respected place in Austin art circles. After a while, she began to teach at the Austin Nature Center, integrating her passion for birds into her craft, hand painting and carving feather patterns, herons, or fish onto white pots. Lois's life in clay is now spread throughout my home; when I hold a green-feathered cereal bowl, I remember her period of deep depression and loneliness. When I press hand soap from the beige carved dispenser, I think of the chronic fatigue that plagued her when it was being kiln-fired. Lois's journey was, and is, a fundamental part of my world.

Little Lois in her ten-gallon-cowboy-hat
Lo in her pottery studio
Lois as Annie Oakley for Halloween

Dave-One and Lo eventually moved out to hill country, near Lake Travis, to a town so small it could barely be called a village. Dave had been hired as the caretaker of the Audubon Bird Sanctuary, where, behind their tin can trailer home, they sidestepped the rattlesnake pit and watched hawks in Live Oaks draped with Spanish moss. Lois listened to hummingbirds' flitting reminder to fill their empty feeders with red nectar for tiny feasts, as she threw pots beside them. She could stand still for what seemed like forever, waiting for a bird to come close. If she didn't know what genus or species it was, out came her tattered field guide, which she'd pour through until she was sure of what she was seeing. Birds flocked to Lois as, with a whispered, "Pshhh, Pshhh, Pshhh," she called them toward her, waiting patiently until they approached to see what this big bird was all about.

Lois split her time as potter and nature advocate, giving speeches at City Council meetings to save Barton Creek and stop overdevelopment of the still-wild surrounds of Austin. She built a mini-rainforest booth for street fairs. Kids would go inside and make masks designed to mimic the endangered Golden-cheeked Warbler and Black-capped Vireo. Lois would teach them the unique antics and calls of each bird. Together they'd squawk, dance, prance, and pick at the dirt, becoming birds of a feather together. She instilled a love for nature in those city-sidewalk kids. But even with all that passion and purpose, she still cowered when Dave-One yelled and stomped and stabbed her with mean words. I started to see that Lois, too, had chosen a man with critical, perfectionist qualities like Dad. She, too, was repeating the patterns of her childhood and could no more break free from them than I could. No matter how much she complained to me about Dave's temper, she could not leave him. And like the days when we were little and our dad ranted over some perceived slight, when Dave threw a tantrum, she withdrew into herself until the storm passed. I watched the drama from the sidelines, sad to see her light grow dimmer little by little.

The Pedestal Crumbles

I was witness to Dave One's blowups and Lo's meltdowns. Every few days, something would pull the trigger, and Dave would go off like shotgun spatter. Lo scurried like a little bird out to her studio, where she stayed trapped like the tiny hummingbird she'd once rescued. But she could not save herself; she was a bundle of nerves, fears, and anxieties. She worried about mold in the carpet. She worried about money. She worried about pollution and the world ending. Like that little girl prematurely pushed out of the nest and still scared of doctors, Lois regressed. Her worry wore out her kidneys and adrenal glands. She was diagnosed as hypoglycemic. The sugars in fruit were impossible for her to tolerate—as if she could no longer take in sweetness of any kind. We've wondered, in years since, whether that was when cancer cells started to grow in her brain. Though we'll never really know, I feel certain that, during that time, Lois was drying up inside.

Being around Lois and Dave was like walking through mud—the kind that sticks to your boots so that each step gets heavier and thicker until it's impossible to walk at all. When I pulled up to their tiny trailer perched off the dirt road, I was relieved if Dave was out pulling stumps or fixing fence posts. Lois was visibly more relaxed when he was gone, and I often timed my visits for when he'd be away so we could talk freely; I implored her to pull herself out of that mud, but she could not. Her body and spirit were breaking down, and Lois had become someone I didn't recognize. It broke my heart. Impatient with Lois's lack of action on her own behalf, I slowly started pulling away from her, putting a wall around my heart so that I wouldn't have to feel her pain—or mine. *Where was the Lois I idolized?* It dawned on me that, ironically, she had become someone I no longer wanted to be.

Wisdom of the Body

While Lo was deep in misery, I had my own dark night of the soul. Like Lois, I'd been struggling with a painful relationship that I tried unsuccessfully to leave. When I came down with diverticulitis (a colon infection that gave me painful constipation peppered with bouts of explosive diarrhea), I sought out a holistic healer. It turned out that letting go in my colon helped me let go of my emotions, and I ended the relationship for good. As my body (and life) healed, I decided to follow a deeper dream instead of staying stuck in my own mud of broken relationships. I went to Kripalu Center in the beautiful Berkshire Mountains of Lenox, Massachusetts, where I trained as a massage therapist. I met fellow seekers and teachers—people I bonded with and looked up to but with whom I had no history or baggage. I was free to become me.

Once when I had bronchitis—coughing until I thought my guts would fly out of my mouth—I lay on the massage table, fully clothed, while gentle hands were laid on my chest and a soft voice gently encouraged me to peek inside my lungs. I saw a golden wheat field, which reminded me of Lawrence, Kansas. Images of the small town on the prairie, where I'd once lived, called up memories of my good friend Susan, who'd died a few years prior. I began sobbing uncontrollably. As my body led me into delayed mourning, I fully let it fly, wailing my sorrow on that massage table where it felt so, so good to be so, so sad. When I'd tapped out my tears, I took stock of my body. After having lain in my bed coughing for days, unable to speak and barely able to breathe, I had become (from that moment and forever after) bronchitis-free. My body took me into a healing crisis so that by expressing my denied grief, beyond healing my lungs, I felt lighter than I'd felt in a hundred years. I felt closer to Susan—and myself, too.

Reticent to leave Kripalu, I became a full-time resident bodyworker there for two years. On my massage table, people delivered up images of hurt, love, hope, and sorrow. As their stories unfolded, knots dissolved, and tendons untangled. I'd invite clients to listen deeply while I'd touch, whispering guiding questions that helped them work through confusion as their body delivered insight and wisdom. I marveled at how our bodies are like symbolic books, telling the story of a whole life through the right-brained language of imagination. By the time I left Kripalu a few years later, I'd been initiated into the healing arts and knew myself as a Healer with a capital H instead of as an Artist like Lois. Most importantly, I began to know myself as a woman on her own path. I'd transformed. When a dear friend nicknamed me Lynnie and his syrupy southern drawl slowly turned it into Lily, I let it stick. It felt like the me I was on the inside.

The Green-Eyed Monster

I moved back to Baltimore and established the Body-Mind Wellness Center, where I practiced the laying on of hands, taught meditation, guided groups in self-study, and created ceremonial rites of passage for personal growth. Lo, too, was exploring the body-mind connection, albeit through increasingly challenging symptoms. Around the time her body gave out from Chronic Fatigue Syndrome, she finally left Dave-One for good. After fourteen years of an emotionally abusive relationship, she was free but physically depleted and emotionally exhausted. Alone, depressed, and sick, she stopped playing soccer and holed up in her tiny apartment in Travis Heights. She tried to reclaim her soul. When she visited Baltimore, my parents said, "Lily will fix her." Alternately inflated and deflated by this expectation, I thought, *I can't fix her; she has to fix herself!* Still, she'd come to my studio, where we'd talk, my hands on her heart. She'd cry, my hands on her belly. She'd shake and rattle her teeth as she released fears stored in every cell of her body, one of my hands tenderly placed on her forehead. I held her and cared for her, while inside I couldn't feel anything. I was cut off. My heart was ensconced in a protective wall, closed and tight. I reached out my hand as family should and because my parents expected and demanded it of me. As different as I felt from her, we'd both cho-sen men who would reflect our deeply ensconced, almost hidden unworthiness right back at us. Hanging on my own hook down there in the underworld, resentment festered. *How dare she be flawed? How dare she!*

Since returning to Baltimore, I'd been taking a series of work-shops and had found a community, as if I'd come home to a circle, a metaphorical neighborhood of folks with whom I felt known, loved, and respected. The Body-Mind Wellness Center was boom-ing and my place in the world solidifying. But I'd also just moved in with Burch, who immediately traipsed off to Italy with his wine and foodie friends. Leaving me to unpack our new home alone, he revealed the pattern of narcissism that would continue throughout our relationship. Despite my best intentions, I was still creating relationships that were mirrors of pain, not love. I found myself more alone than ever and realized how much I'd needed my dad as a little girl. What a deep groove his perfectionist presence and ener-getic absence had created in my being. And Lois had helped carve it even deeper with her criticism. I was right in the thick of discov-ering these wounds when Sally, who'd joined me in the workshop circle, signed Lois up for a weekend course where the three of us would be together for a three-and-a-half-day intensive. Oh Boy!

During that workshop, in one lightening flash, the green wrath of envy flared, and every inadequacy I'd ever known with Lois boiled up like bile in my throat. It was games night—an innocu-ous time of play— when Lois had joyfully jumped out in front of her clan of chickens, turning into the most realistic, head-pecking, tail feather–shaking replica of a chicken any of us had ever seen. As the room burst into gleeful applause, I was overcome with terror. Everyone would surely love Lois more than me. The green-eyed monster had me by the short and curlies. I was filled with dread as jealousy and buried rage erupted. Afterward, I tried telling her about it, but instead clumsily burst out, "I hated you being there!"

Her automatic reflex was as if I'd punched her in the gut, her fragile body contracting into itself. I was consumed with guilt, which only served to fuel my anger. The gates of Hades had been opened, and I couldn't stop myself. I vomited years of vitriol. Unable to see my pain, she struck back, too, accusing me of abandoning her when she needed me most. The tables turned upside down and inside out as we went back and forth with righteous indignation of how we'd each been hurt. There was one moment, as we walked the sandy shores of Liberty Reservoir, when we rose out of the argument and noticed how old and familiar the fight felt. But we were unable to hold that awareness and descended right back into battle. *Hear me! See me!* My mute self suddenly awakened and demanded that someone, that *Lois*, would see what had been roiling underneath the warm touch of my hands onto her body.

We could not stop. We kept yelling, shouting, stalking, pacing, and pointing the finger, neither of us able to hear the other. We stopped talking, we glared, and the love between us shattered. In that quiet moment, I sliced into her with words I had no idea were in me. "That's it! I can be your sister, but I can't be your friend." I'd done it. I'd broken up with her. Years of feeling the victim—the spring curl, the cheese curls, Corry, being less than—grew like a cloud of fog between us. I'm not proud to say it, but it didn't matter to me that I was kicking her while she was down, that I knew she felt friendless and alone, or that she was hurting. It was a pretty bad split-up since Lois thought of me as her best friend. I'd rejected her—as she had done with me when we were little. All I knew right then was my own pain. I'd pushed her as hard and as far away as I could. I wish I could take that day back or live it over again with more kindness. Like a teenager who says the most horrible things to her mother, trying to find her way through adolescence into womanhood, I was pushing against Lois with all my strength that I might find out who I was. When I offer compassion to that younger Lily, I'm able to see that the violent tearing between us was a necessary death—one without which a new beginning would have never been possible.

Truce

One tumultuous year later, my relationship with Burch ended. It was the last straw in my string of failed attempts to find love. Lois and I had formed a cool truce under the veneer of our family closeness. Though neither of us felt good about the absence of depth or authenticity, neither were we able to break out of it. Admittedly, I was comfortable with the distance, finally breathing my own air. I started seeing her through judgmental eyes—comparing, comparing, comparing. She was weak; I was strong. She was anxious; I was calm. She was scared; I was brave. Little by little, the judgments built a higher and higher wall between us, which allowed me to start forming a separate, unique identity. But in spite of our breakup, we both held onto a thread of our former relationship, neither letting go completely.

Then, just before I turned forty, I moved to California, where I lived in a postage-stamp-sized studio. My fortieth birthday felt like a major rite of passage into adulthood, but I had barely a penny to my name, no job, and no intimate community. I felt small, nothing like an adult, and I was frightened and lonely. When I opened the color-coded "birthday-in-a-box" from Lo and Sally, I followed Lois's handwritten directions to first blow up the balloons, which had phrases like, "We love you!" and "Happy Birthday—You're FORTY!!" and "Go For It!" written on them. The second instruction was to bat them around the room, which got me laughing, but after the third directive—tossing confetti and yelling happy birthday—I collapsed in tears. Sisterly love burst out of that box, but I was the only one in the room. Trying to pretend it was a festive moment didn't really work. Though the gift was from both of them, I knew the inspiration for that box was Lo's, and I wanted her there with me. The truth was, I missed her. As cancer later showed me, my relationship with Lois really, really mattered.

Three

Life Is a Schoolroom

I had this thought the other day…just as we are gestated inside the mother's body before being birthed out into the world through the root chakra, our manifested lives are like a gestation in the body of the earth, where we grow in physical, mental, and soulful ways. And when the right amount of growth for a Soul has occurred, death is a birth into another plane of existence, one that we can't see with our current consciousness.

—Sally

Falling in Love

While I was alone and lonely in my little studio, Lois, on the other hand, had met David Akard. Though at first we thought of him as Dave-Two, eventually the Myers clan adopted him whole-heartedly, and he became just Dave. Used to love without a lot of fluff, he was wide-eyed at the Myers way of kissin' on the lips but over time he lapped up the warmth of our clan and sidled up to our outspoken ways. He spoke with a charming drawl; it was just the slightest southern twang, most likely inherited from his mother's Nebraskan and his daddy's Oklahoman roots. Dave and Lois met in Stacey Park over volleyball, though Dave actually met Lo's underwear—her bright freak flag—before he met her. Since she lived at the edge of the park where Dave walked his dog, he'd often noticed the multicolored panties she unabashedly clipped to the clothesline, musing, "Now there's a gal who ain't afraid of color!" Once he put the girl together with the underwear, he was intrigued. But when he basked in the glow of her big smile and discovered Lo's creative spirit, he was smitten.

I first met Dave over breakfast at Lo's favorite restaurant, Magnolia Grill. I thought he was cute, especially the rattail creeping down his back. He stopped to chat then moved on, and Lo leaned conspiratorially across the table to whisper, "He has a crush on me." I said, "Go for it!" They grew slowly into friendship on evening walks through the park, and Dave-Two fell in love with Lois Joy long before she was ready. Since he'd been married and amicably divorced, years before, his baggage was long unpacked, while hers was still in the suitcase. But over time, she came to trust his depth of character. When Lo went back to school to get her master's in environmental education, Dave took a backseat, accepting minimal together time without a fuss—no sulking! When uncertainty reined in response to his repeated marriage proposals, his absence of emotional outbursts caught her by surprise. At parties she could talk to men without jealous recriminations. Dave-Two never reacted like Dave-One had; he didn't yell at her when she cried or rage over her extroverted activities. And beyond all that, he was funny. He had a magical way of lightening the mood of challenging moments. When Don (Sally's husband) grumbled and groused over a technological conundrum, Dave swallowed him in a bear hug until Don surrendered his frustration in a fit of red-faced laughter. At my parents' fiftieth wedding anniversary, Dave donned a goofy plaid golf cap to heighten the silliness, then sat up late into the candlelit night with we three sisters, a steady support emanating toward Lois as we vented, sorting out clashes of personality. Dave's Siddha Yoga practices of chanting and meditation developed a great gentleness in him. He once told me that meditating every day was his way of working through years of accumulated "stuff." It seemed to work; he appeared to have a well of calm patience that he'd dug deep. Dave-Two passed all of Lois's tests; his love wore her down until she finally let go, opening her heart and succumbing to love. True love.

Dave, Dave, Dave

In spite of lamenting that his family used sarcasm and humor to deal with difficult feelings, Dave loved his laughing, game-playing, roughhousing family. Cut from Midwestern stock, his large family (three brothers: Perry, Jack, and Randy and two sisters: Lu and Jodee) was centered in the Church of Christ. It was a rigorous tradition. Tenets that forbid dancing or swimming with members of the opposite sex were hard for Dave to accept. Definitely no tobacco or alcohol. Even though his parents, Jack and Gene, let the kids swim coed at the local pool, when it came to in-front-of-the-congregation confessions of wrongdoing, they followed protocol. That rankled Dave's sensibilities. As a teen, he defected altogether when he couldn't come to terms with the belief that only members of their sect would make it into heaven. Instead, he grew his hair long, became a vegetarian, and started practicing meditation through Siddha Yoga, a tradition born in India and brought to the West by Swami Muktananda in the 1970s. The teachings, now carried out by a woman affectionately called Gurumayi, center on recognizing the divinity in everything and everyone, including oneself. Siddha Yoga, as I saw Dave live it, is a path to an open heart.

Dave's older brothers, Perry and Jack, could never fathom Dave's meditative path. As if becoming a vegetarian were a personal assault on their spirituality, they rejected his spiritual path altogether. As a result, sensitive little Davey and an older David didn't feel seen or truly known by them. He was as deeply wounded by this, as I was in my rift with Lois. In self-protection, he rejected them back. His younger siblings, Jodee and Randy, were less strident, though their ambivalence toward Dave's spiritual life also wedged some small distance. But Dave's Big Sister, Lu, was where he found *home.* I can't recount how often Dave said, "There's nothin' like a sister," and I knew this referred to the depth of love between him and his Lucy. As the two sensitive ones, they were a team, united in protection from the sometimes-abusive older brothers. They *belonged* to one another, linked "like an appendage to my own soul, like an arm or leg," according to Lu. Though their spiritual paths differed, in their hearts, they were one.

Dave, Dave, Dave: with his sister, Lu and his mom, Gene

Dave lived with Lu and her family for a time; that's when he built the Good Earth Cafe, nestled in the back of the local health-food store in Sherman, Texas. He baked hearty-grained buns each night, into the wee morning hours, upon which he served wholesome, pure and simple foods, from peanut-butter–and–banana sandwiches to hefty bean burgers. And though the Good Earth Cafe had a sweet following, he left it behind when he moved to Austin. He was drawn to the creative cultural enclave of the Texas capital, where he followed his dream of becoming a social worker and had the good fortune to meet and eventually marry Lois.

The Thirteenth Fairy

They married beneath a *chuppah* built of fresh bamboo poles and plumes of pampas grasses, overlooking a lush green river valley and dedicated their marriage to a spiritual union in which love was the sweeping star. Love, love, and more love!

Lois and Dave's wedding

They asked me to read something during the ceremony: "Love is the light of spirit shown through the eyes of the one(s) we adore..." I secretly thought of it as overly sweet, like saccharin. *It's too la-la, too love and lighty for my taste*, I thought, having grown cynical in my tiny, single studio. Yet true to the paradox of me and Lo, I entertained the idea, *If Lo can finally get married, maybe I can too!* But when Dave stomped on the cup at their wedding—Jewish tradition requires the groom to smash a cup as a symbolic act to ward away bad luck—instead of breaking, it sank into the soft grass. I was sure it was a bad omen.

As evening fell, the torches were lit, joyous dancing began, and Sally and I gathered with Lo for a photo behind the wedding cake. Underneath my sugary-love smile, I kept comparing. I thought, *We are so different! Where is the shadow in all this?* But Lois had surrendered to love, and in truth, it made me wonder whether I, too, was lovable. All my internal pushing and pulling was just another expression of how I was bound to Lois, and it drew the thread tighter around us.

I came to think of the glass sunken into the grass as a visitation from the thirteenth fairy. In the tale, the fairy places a curse on festivities because she wasn't invited to the ceremony. She represents the shadow, the unexpected forces of life, that come during the grandest moments to disrupt the status quo, offering potential for growth cloaked as disaster. I couldn't shake the feeling that the thirteenth fairy, the shadow of love, had entered the party after all. I worried about it so much that when I eventually married, I told Seth, "You better stomp the shit out of that glass!" And he did; we were taking no chances.

About a year after they were married, Dave and Lo moved to the little town of Buda, south of Austin, where their limestone-brick house backed up to woods filled with birds, deer, and wildflowers. My first visit there came after the curse of the thirteenth fairy had taken shape in Lois's brain. A tumor had revealed itself like the big bang while she was visiting her best friend, Ellen, on Memorial Day morning. As Ellen tells it, Lois started stuttering, saying, "Lily used to say, Lily used to say, Lily used to say…ahhhh…gaaahhhh," and Ellen was trying to figure out "why Lily would make that sound" when she realized that Lois was having a seizure. Immediately, Ellen slid over and loosely hugged Lois, crying, "Is your tongue all right? Is your tongue all right?" Lo could hear but couldn't answer, even though she later told us she'd wanted say, "YES! My tongue is still in my mouth!" Then she blacked out in Ellen's arms. When she opened her eyes again, Lois muttered, "I'm so g-r-o-g-g-y." When Ellen asked her if she knew what had just happened, her brain cells chugged, searching for clues, until finally she whispered, "Oh, yes, I remember. I just had a grand-mal seizure…Did I foam at the mouth?" Ellen nodded and held up her nice white washcloth as she forced herself to smile. Thus began Lois's fourteen-year cancer journey in the spirit-filled embrace of her closest friend.

I'd learned about the seizure when I answered a call from my mother. I briskly said, "I'm about to teach a class." Her response, "Call me back when you have time," dripped with an uncharacteristic foreboding that reverberated in my skin. Pushing briskness aside, I answered, "Wait, what's wrong? Tell me. Now." I gazed out the window, unseeing, stunned by her response. "Lois has brain cancer." I listened as Mom explained that Lois was going to have her skull cut open and the tumor removed in a matter of days, that she wanted M&M there, that Sally would join as soon as she could, and that Lois was ambivalent about my coming. My insides rumbled, and my mind went numb. Since my relationship with Lois was tenuous, the threat of her death stirred the pot at the center of my being. Sludge from the bottom of our clan soup started rising—too many conflicting feelings to count. I went on to teach the class in a dreamlike state, though my world had just shifted on its axis. I looked out at that changed-forever world through eyes that could only see a murky fog of lost connections from the past and fear of what would—or would not—be possible in the future.

There was no hiding it now; Lois and I were carrying out the Myers tradition of family disharmony and dissonance. I was heartbroken to realize I'd been excluded from a moment of great import. It was unfathomable that I would not be there! Looking death in the eye, I saw how deeply I loved my sister—messy, crappy unresolved hurts and all. I wanted to be by her side. Cautiously, Lois finally agreed that I could visit after she was home from surgery. Relieved, I entered their new limestone house to find my sister tiny and wan in her bed, head bandaged in a huge turban of white gauze with a gemstone Dad had pinned at the center. I tiptoed directly into her room and crawled into bed beside her. She opened her eyes and silently welcomed me by reaching her arms out to me. Weeping, I tucked myself into my Big Sister's arms—familiar, known arms. Silently, Lois and I looked deeply into each other's eyes, and the frozen fortress around my heart melted. We each whispered a tender "I love you…"

I'd met and fallen in love with Seth one month before the fireworks went off in Lois's brain. While psychologists often say that women marry their fathers, when I met Seth, I thought, *I'm finally in love with my mother!* A poet and writer, his well-developed emotional intelligence far surpassed any man I'd ever known. We'd met over lunch, orchestrated by my cousin Sandy, who'd gotten close to Seth after his lifetime partner, Cynthia, had passed away. It was far from a chemistry-filled love-at-first-sight meeting, but after a long afternoon of deep talk that turned into the longest date ever, I knew he was the one. While Seth continued to mourn Cynthia's passing, our love grew organically. We entered each other's hearts as if we had no choice in the matter. He changed the way I saw the world; I was just softer. I felt more cherished than I had since living in the red brick house, and so it was easier to love. Seth supported me through Lo's first cancer episode as an experienced cancer caregiver, which deepened our bond. Then I filled him in on all my stories about Lois.

Turbaned Lois after brain surgery
Lois embraced by love: Sally on left and Lily on right

Truth Time

His kind viewpoint was a breath of fresh air when, several months into her recovery, we all convened in Baltimore. Family reunions are often a petri dish for the unconscious waltz of the family trance, and ours was no exception. Since M&M's house was small, we planned to sack out on mattresses in an empty unit of my aunt's apartment building. After a warm and cozy wine-soaked evening, we tumbled into the crisp night, the damp November air chilling our necks beneath woolly scarves. Chaos reigned as we tried to figure out who'd go in who's car and to the store for forgotten toothbrushes and morning coffee and milk. My own chill deepened when Lois shouted, "I don't want Lily to get there first because she'll take the best bed!" Her words landed like a punch in my gut. Remembering the many times I'd slept on the floor while everyone else got beds or in the open basement while others got bedrooms with doors, I was drawn into a stunned silence. Age-old barbs rose to the surface and stung with this unspoken accusation of greediness. Feeling misunderstood and maligned, I simply withdrew—mute—as I had in childhood, to soothe my suffering in private. But this time it was different; I was not alone. With Seth beside me, wrapping me in love, I saw the dilemma through his eyes. For the first time, I understood that Lois and I both held a shroud of projections in front of the other; neither of us could see the other clearly. The next day, when Lois told me she wanted to visit me in Oakland, and spend time with just the two of us, I was still hurt. And nervous. Nevertheless, I agreed.

When Lois arrived the following spring, I expected admonishment, but as we sat on the couch in my living room, light streaming through the picture window, she surprised me. "Since the cancer, I've realized it's best to tell people how I feel about them and not wait. I love you, but I feel distant from you. I don't want that any more. I've been hurting in our relationship. I timidly let you back in when you came to take care of me after my brain surgery, and I think you let me back in, then, too." In truth, I'd still been holding her at arm's length, afraid to let anything in, even her love. I was scared, and my body went on high alert, pouring adrenaline into my brain as if I were being threatened. The never-before-said hurts swirled, unformed and wordless, like wind between my ears. Then she said, "What happened between us felt like a lover's breakup that went on and on. I've never let go of the pain or forgiven you for it. You were my dearest friend, and when you pushed me away, I was shocked. I've been upset all these years. But I miss you. I want to be close again." She reminded me of the time we drove to Sal and Don's farm while I taught her the Sufi song: *"Ish-ka-a-lah-ma-boud-lay-la…All I ask of you is forever to remember me, as loving you…"* We wanted to sing it in rounds, but neither of us could keep our own part going once the other chimed in. We'd tried it every which way, each time getting more and more tangled until we were laughing so hard we literally couldn't see. Hysterical and blind, I had to pull the car to the side of the road. When she told me, "I miss that kind of openness with you, Lil," my limited reality broke open. My entire angle was based on Lois as the rejecting perpetrator of my damaged self. This compassionate approach threatened the status quo of that story. I'd so fully crafted a tale of victimization and distance that to hear the caring, vulnerable words coming from her mouth frightened me. Like a door painted shut, opening my heart was not so easy. Behind that door was a circus performer spinning plates atop a stick. With one hand, I was spinning the realities of cancer and potential death while, with the other, I spun my own lingering hurts. My chest tightened as I tried with all my might to open, but trying to open is not the same as *being* open. The years of unspoken words rose up, as did my rage for the self-loathing she'd instilled in me, and I knew I had to speak my own truth, not just listen to hers. I opened my mouth and somehow managed to express my anger without dumping it. I described how she hurt me growing up, how painful it was to follow behind her at school, how I could never measure up to her standards, being so flawed I wasn't allowed to touch her bed or her hair. Then the big doozy came out: she should never even have *asked* me if she could sleep with Corry. She was my Big Sister, my idol. How could she have done that? I told her about my jealousy. About the green bile. About how I didn't feel lovable. This time she listened. She asked questions, and it felt good to be heard. I wasn't ready to forgive, but I was ready to consider it. Lois and I wanted to be free of the hurts that had passed between us, and I knew that forgiveness was the key to that freedom. The next day she told me, "I'm glad we talked openly yesterday. I felt your love through the way you communicated, even though you were talking about being discounted and hurt." I felt my protective wall breaking down, and as my frozen heart melted, forgiveness flowed along with it.

I learned that just saying the words "I forgive you" isn't enough. It didn't instantly resolve the subtle judgments I carried in the privacy of my own head. It didn't stop Lois's reactive blurting "I just don't trust you!" much later when it came to handling our parents' finances. I held those words against her, thinking, *That proves it; she doesn't respect me—the hell with her.* But we kept working on forgiveness, talking things through. Lois was often vulnerable instead of attacking, saying things like, "I'm just scared. I didn't mean that. I do trust you." And I started to believe her.

Over time I've come to see that, beyond Lois and Lily, larger ancestral patterns were playing out between us. Our critical, hard-to-please father carried his own father's wounds, who in turn carried the devastation of his family's homeland. Down through the generations, love in our family has often looked like criticism. I think about how wounds are passed down from one generation to the next, through both nature and nurture. When I think of this, I am reminded of the biblical phrase, *"The sins of the father shall be visited upon the son."* The phrase, I realize now, is a reminder that all of us carry out the hurts of our ancestors. It was natural for Lois and I to love each other in the same way our forebears had, though none of it was conscious at the time. Our great-grandparents' unexpressed grief had been watered down into habits of criticism and perfectionism, but that energy had to go somewhere. Just trying to survive, the luxury of grieving hadn't been possible for them. Since rejected or submerged grief easily redirects into anger, I've often wondered whether their experience of persecution created the perpetrator and victim consciousness in our DNA. *Did Lois and I, in our close relationship, pick up those patterns?* Without a single doubt, Lois and I loved each other, but that did not stop us from projecting our wounds onto one another. Perhaps we carried the patterns in an attempt to heal them for our whole family. Healthier than holding back, truth telling was building a new foundation, brick by shaky brick. It took more than a decade to build, but we'd begun crafting it with deep honesty that day on the couch. Though we couldn't change our ancestors' experience, forgiveness was the path to heal the habits we'd inherited from them. We'd stir the pot a thousand times more before finding our way back to what ultimately mattered most: real, genuine, unfettered love.

The Dream

Nearly a year after her first brain surgery, the impact of cancer and treatment was still an ever-present guest at Lois's table. Cognitive functions were returning slowly, but Lois did not feel whole; she felt unsafe in the world and struggled to make sense of what had happened to her. As we walked the soft needle-laden trail in the Oakland hills, Lois asked me to help her work a dream. She told it, saying, "I'm walking in the mountains in a large expanse of deep, white, glistening snow. I'm searching for a sacred white snake but can't find it. Suddenly I'm in a pit of quicksand, swirling down, sinking deeper and deeper. The scene shifts, and I'm gazing down from above at a beautiful, still, blue mountain lake." The images washed over us as we settled into a quiet rhythm, the silence of giant redwoods weaving a calming cape over us. Tenderly, we unlocked the symbols, as one does when listening deeply to a poem. The white snake symbolized her sacred path—one for which she was searching—and the shedding of layers required in order to grow. The glistening white snow was her inner spiritual terrain—a place of exquisite, pristine beauty. The tall mountains reminded her of a Nepalese trek into the farthest reaches of heaven, and the quicksand symbolized her descent into the earth, into matter, cancer, and the underworld of her psyche. The Lois who was gazing down at the still, blue lake from above was not embodied, instead it was her expanded consciousness. Lois interpreted the blue lake as representing the blue pearl, which she defined as a symbol of transcendence.

The depth of this dream reverberated through us both. We understood that brain cancer was taking her on a soul journey, the quicksand pulling ground from beneath her at every level, initiating her into the far reaches of her own, innate being. The process would be transformational, like a snake shedding layer upon layer of skin. Cancer was to be Lois's sacred journey of transcendence—a spiritual awakening. I also knew, but didn't say it then, that cancer would take my sister's life. Instead, I said soberly, "Lo, I think you're going to have a long and hard road ahead of you with this cancer." As I felt the truth of those words, love replaced mistrust, restoring the texture of friendship in our sisterly fabric.

Cancer Ping-Pong

Four years later, we gathered for a cousin's Bar Mitzvah in Tucson. Lois was awaiting the five-year mark to formally celebrate remission, but she was finally functioning normally. When she asked us to join her after dinner, we crammed into M&M's small hotel suite where, with her newly characteristic bluntness, she said, "Dave has cancer." As we absorbed the blow, she told us the whole story. He'd been to a doctor for blood in his stool, who'd said, "No worries; it's just hemorrhoids. You just have to get used to a little blood." He coped, then returned, intuiting a bigger issue, and said, "It's too much blood." After more tests, while Lois was camping in Big Bend, Dave came home from leading a meditation class for prison inmates. Alone, he faced a blinking answering machine, then fell to his knees when he heard the disembodied voice saying that his colonoscopy revealed cancer. Heartbroken, scared, and lonely for Lo's support, he called Lu, at nearly midnight, and they cried together. Lo told us, "My heart hurt when I pictured him alone hearing the news." We had a hard time fathoming that both of them had gotten cancer.

I loved Dave and was grateful he had helped Lois's heart to heal, but with the long history of hurt between Lo and me, some mistrust lay between us. He was cautious about letting me in and I was equally careful in return. Because of that distance, the story of Dave's biopsy and ensuing surgery is blurry for me. Dave's mom, Lu, his brother, Perry, Sally and Ellen were there for his surgery, and distance or not, I remember well the post-surgery report we got from Lois: stage-four cancer, eighteen or twenty-two lymph nodes affected. Dave's cancer had penetrated portions of his muscular and lymph system so that, in addition to the surgical removal of more than a foot of his colon and a section of his rectum, a colostomy bag was implanted. A long haul was in store. Dave knew that his resolve would be tested, and it was. He drew upon his ancestral inheritance: his mother's abiding faith. She honored Dave's spirituality from a deep well of her own, and Dave treasured her trust. He quoted her words again and again, "Now it's time to rest upon your bed of prayers," as he acknowledged feeling more vulnerable and dependent than he had since his early childhood days. He suffered intensely from a series of complications, followed by a year of hard-core chemo and radiation. On his last day of chemo, Lois orchestrated a deluge of flowers from friends, family, and coworkers to celebrate the passage. As he weathered his last pass through nausea and vomiting, he walked into a house filled (even the bathtub!) with color. He said that the side effects receded as love infused his cells, all the way down to his toes. It had been a wild ride, and Lois had risen to the challenge, riding with him through every unexpected dip and twist of the track.

After fifteen months of treatment and one final surgery to remove the colostomy bag and "reattach his plumbing," they reached a major turning point. It was done. Dave's last hospital visit. As they drove from Houston to Austin, they imagined that they would rest and return to life as normal—or at least to their new normal. Then, on that celebratory ride, as if in a game of cancer ping-pong, Lois started having breakthrough seizures, five years after the first one, in Ellen's arms. Unfortunately, they were not just signs of stress, as we'd hoped. They were outright symptoms of a second brain tumor. Lois and Dave reversed roles. Again. A close friend of mine kept repeating, "What are the odds? What are the odds?" It was uncanny how Lois and Dave shared cancer—back and forth, to and fro, one after the other. Somehow they survived the rigor of relentless illness and toxic medicines that made them sicker than ever. They grappled with depression and dramatic emotional episodes. Lois went from a full time job to part time, then onto disability. Yet they emerged from every setback every time, choosing to put their limited energy toward living and loving. A friend told me how blown away he was when Dave said, "My one regret with my fatigue was not being as present to Lo." Lois told me that she felt she'd been "spared in order to care for Dave." As they climbed each hurdle, with both grace and grit, their love for one another grew.

Relay for Life

Lois said that before her first surgery, "Getting on that gurney was the hardest and scariest thing I've ever done in my life."

Then, during the surgery, while still under anesthesia, she'd had a revelatory experience telling us, "I remember the feeling of love all around me and realized that the universe was *made of love.*" *Love is all that matters* became her mantra; it was what she held onto when she went for her second brain surgery. As Lois searched for lessons she was "supposed to learn" and tried to make meaning out of cancer's meaninglessness, she leaned into love. Though she was far from perfect, Lois practiced choosing love over fear. As love became the guiding principle of their lives, both Lois and Dave were determined NOT to be the victims in their own story. They believed that learning the life lessons taught by cancer would open doors to a healing miracle.

Believing that their bodies were expressions of their spirit, Lois and Dave sought to open their hearts more fully. Lois held firmly to the notion that "body, mind, and spirit are one" and examined her thoughts and attitudes, hoping that changing one aspect would simultaneously heal the rest. Drawing upon the depth of their philosophy, they both called upon a wealth of resources, taking care to address both physicality and spirituality. Lois went for regular acupuncture treatments, and they changed their already rigorous diets to include macrobiotic eating (balancing yin-and-yang foods for optimum balance) and ayurvedic principles (an East-Indian yogic healing approach). They joined cancer support groups and found a therapist whose special focus on life-threatening illness deepened their journey. Just like her dream had foreshadowed, her body and its dis-ease became Lo's search for transformation, a *cancer journey* that was much more than mere illness. Lois and Dave crafted their story in e-mails, feeding their gathered tribe, who consumed them voraciously, as manna. We marveled at how they turned their suffering into a path of growth, publicly bushwhacking a trail through the thickets. Each story touched a chord, each dip was balanced by faith, and each blow was countered with gratitude.

Finally, nine years after Lois's first brain tumor, they were both cancer-free. I wanted to shout, "Freeze!" I'd started to see the cancer for the quicksand that it was, and I wanted to savor the moment. Celebrating cancer freedom is exactly what Dave and Lois did.

Dave celebrating the end of yearlong chemotherapy treatments
Dave and Lois with friends at Buda's Relay for Life Fundraiser

They'd been asked to be keynote speakers at a *Relay for Life* fundraiser sponsored by The American Cancer Society. I know they felt honored as survivors to be part of the Luminaria Ceremony—a sacred service where people gather to honor ancestors and support loved ones fighting cancer. The event took place amid lots of hustle-bustle on Buda's high-school track, with well over a thousand people present. After darkness fell, everything stopped. Lights went off. People sensed the sanctity of the moment and became silent. It was pitch black, except for the full moon and hundreds of luminarias—paper bags lit by candles sitting in a bed of sand—lining the track and illuminating the night. A lone bagpiper dressed in full Scottish regalia played "Amazing Grace" as he slowly walked around the track, emptied of walkers.

The speech they gave is exactly what I wanted for them—a concrete expression of lessons learned and a newfound lease-on-life energy. From the beginning, they'd wanted to write their cancer story; Lois, especially, talked often about "our book." The following speech is as close as they got to being the tellers of their own tale.

DAVE: "We've been asked to talk about our journey with cancer. We've both been cancer patients; we've been each other's caregiver; and at times we've been both patient and caregiver at the same time. Now we're **survivors**. *As difficult as it has all been, we believe it was meant to happen so we'd have an opportunity to learn some life lessons that we've considered blessings in disguise of cancer.*

LOIS: During my first surgery, I sensed love all around me and realized the universe was MADE OF LOVE and that love was all that mattered. This is what helped me to heal from the trauma of the surgery and deal with the emptiness, depression, and hopelessness I felt afterward.

When Dave got stage-four colo-rectal cancer and I became HIS care-giver, I was able to understand his needs intimately. I supported him both physically and emotionally. The most challenging part for me was that I knew I couldn't fix him. That's when I realized caregivers are also co-survivors.

DAVE: During the time I was in treatment, a fellow cancer survivor helped me get in touch with how much I wanted to live. It was a shot in the arm to realize that while God would decide my ultimate fate, my own spirit also played an important part in the outcome. [That helped me find] the will...the desire to beat it.

LOIS: I would never choose brain cancer to learn about myself or to recognize what I need to work on, but it forced me to face my fears and helped me open my heart.

Together, Dave and I learned more about being resolute, living in the present moment, honesty, spirit, and our need for play in our lives. Now I am so aware of the fragility of life and how any one of us can go at any time that it has helped me to realize love in a way that I'm not sure I would have reached otherwise.

DAVE: As a caregiver, the cancer scared me, but the fear began to lose its grip when I talked about it and learned not to hold back or be afraid to say or do the wrong thing. I learned to trust that love always shines through.

During this time, my dear mom said, "David, now it's time to rest on your bed of prayers." These words brought me great comfort as I gained a deeper understanding that, as strong as I tried to be, I didn't have to go it alone. I learned that allowing a friend to do something for me not only lifted my burden, it gave that friend an opportunity to participate in beating the cancer.

Beyond that, my journey through cancer brought me closer to my heart, to the ones I love, and closer to Spirit.

LOIS: Though we realize we are not immune, we are both cancer-free now and living life in our new normal. We each have aftereffects of surgeries and treatments, regular reminders of the cancer that used to inhabit our bodies. Yet, when we look back on our journey, we're also reminded of our blessings, especially the ways in which we were supported by loved ones.

DAVE: We want to close by saying how much this Relay for Life means to us. It is the community's way of saying, we're here to support you, cheer for you, cry with you...to make your *struggle* our *struggle. That's what matters most to us, and in return, we offer thanks and blessings to you all!*

These words were Lois and Dave's way of integrating all they had learned. They'd scoured their souls as they suffered through the ins and outs of cancer and its treatments. By offering their words to the Buda *Relay for Life* community of cancer patients, survivors, and those having lost a loved one, they gave of themselves as they crafted their speech, hoping their story would offer a glimmer of hope to others.

Cancer, as it turned out, was my teacher, too; I was starting, slowly, to accept that "love is all that matters" and to believe that the "blessings of love" that Lois and Dave talked about were real. Like Inanna, both Lois and Dave had been hanging on the cancer hook, and they'd allowed themselves to be changed by it. Their lessons became mine as I walked the *cancer journey* beside them. And I started to think that maybe their marriage commitments about love had not been so *la-la* after all.

75

Section Two

Deepening into Destiny

Dave and I have been incrementally introduced to suffering and an altered lifestyle through cancer, so this newest diagnosis is not so drastic for us; we're just doing cancer <u>together</u> now.

The fact that, in the past, we were taking turns having cancer and now we are diagnosed on the same day seems to be telling us that there is a divine plan. We feel like this is our destiny playing out.

We want to live, but not at the expense of quality of life—a quality WE will determine as we go through this process.

—Lois

Four

The Search

When I was sixteen, it came time for confirmation in my Jewish faith. I took it seriously but didn't believe in the "God sitting on a throne up in the sky." I thought about it a lot, knowing that I couldn't get confirmed without believing in God.

But I figured it out! Or at least began to. I realized that God was a universal energy, which is how God could be everywhere at one time. I was so excited to realize this, I wanted to talk about God with any-one who was willing.

All things seemed sacred to me, from trees, seeds, and even the news-paper (that I sometimes ran over and apologized to) to other animals, to my family, other people, and to the wider realm.

Even now, I feel humbled by it.

—Lois

A Roller Coaster of Love

For those nine cancer-in-tandem years, Lois and I rode a roller coaster, looping from the highs of joyful connection and trust to the lows of misunderstanding, doubt, and suspicion. One of the highs was midway through those years, after her second brain surgery. Lo wanted M&M there, even though their marbles had started coming a little loose. They were still walking, albeit a slow shuffle for Dad, and talking, though much too loud for a post-brain-surgery patient. I knew how frail of mind they were becoming, easily getting mixed up just trying to keep track of a daily schedule, and how vulnerable they were, though they tried to cover it up. I was becoming parent to my parents and worried that the stress of watching their daughter go through her second brain surgery would put them under. And I wanted to protect Dave so he could focus on Lo. I wanted to be of service to all of them. To my great relief, my suggestion to be there, as a comfort and chauffeur to M&M, was welcomed. In this indirect way, I was able to be there for Lo, too.

After the surgery and ICU stay was complete, but before Lo could be released from the hospital, she was required to pee a liter. The nurse placed a portable commode next to the bed and perched Lois dutifully upon it, bladder full and ready to spill. When no waterfall emerged, Lois proposed a trip to the bathroom, which cautious nurses had dictated was too far. So Dave ran some water. No go. He told some bad jokes. Nope. He told some good ones. Still nothing. We tried pushing it outta her—Dave pressed on her back while I pushed on her bladder—insanity! All three of us were giggling; Dave and I almost peed our own pants as we hooted at the three stooges-ness of us. We squeezed her like a lemon, waterworks flying from everywhere but Lo's stubborn bladder. Laughing, poking, prodding, "C'mon, Lo! Pee already!" Finally we agreed to rebel. Sneaking behind the nurse's back, we each took an arm, shuffled her to the real bathroom and just like that, she sat down, peed a quart, and off home we headed.

Within the most dire of circumstances, Lois and I mended the tears in our fabric, which opened doors for Dave and I to bond, too, just in time for my Memorial Day wedding. On that day, beyond a hearty stomping of the crystal glass, Seth and I invited transformation (*and* the thirteenth fairy!) into our union as the sun broke through the clouds. Lo, in her colorful little Guatemalan yarmulke-like pillbox hat covering her shaved head, read from Kahlil Gibran's *The Prophet*, "For even as love crowns you, so shall he crucify you. Even as he is for your growth, so is he for your pruning..." While a black-and-yellow butterfly flitted back and forth over our heads, we exchanged vows, "To love you and to see the divine in you so that each of us may realize our deepest spiritual purpose," which reverberated with meaning. But when the Beatles song trumpeted its message, "All you need is love," bubbles floated to the sky, and we fell into a tearful group hug with Lois and Dave right in the middle.

Moments like this were the top of the roller coaster, but sudden turns took us careening downhill just the same. One of those slides came at the end of the nine years when Lois and Dave were travel-worthy again and came to visit Seth and me in our new home in the Oakland hills. Surrounded by pine and eucalyptus trees, Dave scurried up the hillside for a close-up look at my landscaping while Lo and I stood on level ground and answered his questions about

what was what. "Bay tree: native. Scotch broom: not." Lo filled me
in on healthy habitats. I learned, native species: good; nonnative,
more invasive varieties: bad. We soaked in the hot tub later that
night and went for a long hike the next day, talking and laughing
at nothing in particular while we caught up on our lives. But my
childlike excitement was soon submerged. When Dave went off to
visit friends, and Seth was at work, Lo and I had time to ourselves.
We explored new trails, and I shared some intimate stories from my
recent vision quest. When we returned home and I lay down with
a headache, Lois burst out in a degrading tone, "You have a lot of
STUFF!" Shocked, my quick retort, "But it's really good stuff!" covered the sting of her familiar criticism. Like a turtle, I retreated into
my shell and withdrew my exuberant outstretched heart. I had been
so excited to share my home with her and Dave, and for the first
time in ages, I had opened my heart fully when I shared my sacred
stories with her. Bewildered, I shut down and fell back into the family trance, returning to dutiful hosting rather than loving sisterhood,
waiting out the time, counting the days until she would leave. At the
end of each day, as we curled into each other's arms, I whispered to
Seth each slight, each judgmental comment, each facial expression
that had bit into me.

Yet on the last day of that visit, Lois surprised me when she
rushed tearfully into my arms. She confessed, "I've been judging you
this whole time. When you lay down with that headache, I took it as
rejection." I'd once wondered aloud, with Lois, about whether getting tired or not feeling well around family was a method of pulling
away to meet my needs for autonomy. When Lois admitted that she
interpreted my headache as a ruse for turning away from her, she said,

"I retaliated by rejecting you." *Holy moly, so that's what's been going on!* She ended with a big apology, "I'm so, so sorry." Caught between compassion and frustration, I struggled to find an answer. It was a big step for her to acknowledge something so deeply embedded. But I was angry that she'd been hurtful and turned my words against me; I wondered how it could be safe to share realizations if each admission could so easily turn into rejection. I was frustrated that a whole visit had been lost but relieved that I hadn't been making up those barbs; she *had* been piercing me with negative vibes.

Paradise Lost Is Consciousness Gained

Since Lois's confession was just minutes before she left, we never explored it at length. But we did acknowledge how easily, and without consciously intending to, we sliced deeply into each other. We both had a habit of perceiving criticism in all things, and we both suffered from a persecution complex festering in our DNA, grown from our ancestors' tangible experience of oppression. I imagined how my grandfather instilled certainty that the world was an unsafe and rejecting place into his children. As an immigrant in the United States in the early 1900s, he experienced his fair share of anti-Semitism, reactivating memories of pogroms and Cossacks with swords and torches. Certainly he criticized my dad, and no matter how well intentioned it had been, the habitual perception of persecution was passed down. This dance of love and rejection that Lois and I sashayed in and out of was bigger than just the two of us. That visit was a turning point for me, as I made a conscious choice toward compassion. I started practicing letting go of suspicion right then and there, choosing instead to trust my sister.

And I found that compassion was an amazing thing, spawning forgiveness, then insight. Soon after Lois left, I woke up in the middle of the night with a phrase reverberating through me so strongly that I could not fall back to sleep: *It is one's wholeness that causes one to seek wholeness.* The words echoed through my inner chambers as I lay awake. *I want to know myself as whole.* The story of Adam and Eve eased into my mind and I thought about its symbolism. I realized that when in paradise, before their fall from grace, the myth says that they were unified, unaware of their separateness. As I lay on my back, watching the moon cross the sky through the window over my bed, I pondered: *If eating fruit from the Tree of Knowledge is what caused Adam and Eve to discover their separateness, then it is knowledge (or the mind) that splits them from unity. When they fall from paradise they leave their divinity behind and become human; it's just like being born. As with Adam and Eve, when conscious thought begins we forget that we are One, cutting us off from our essential being. This forgetfulness causes us to believe that we are separate. The loss of that state of Oneness— whatever we were before embodiment—is the wounding thorn in our side, evoking a deep longing to return to that peaceful state.*

Wide awake, I thought about how the story of Adam and Eve is part of the Judeo-Christian creation myth—core mythology for western civilization. As such, it has meaning for the entire culture. I began to think of Adam and Eve's fall as a kind of homelessness. Like Jews forced from little towns in Latvia, Adam and Eve were banished from their homeland. They—the Jews, Adam and Eve, and all of us—are homeless. The fall does not symbolize original *sin*, as it is often interpreted; it is the original *wound* of all humanity. All of us, in whatever form, however consciously or unconsciously, are seeking a return to that existential home. Me, Lois, Seth, Dave. Everyone. Like Pop-Pop estranged from his homeland, this myth told me that we are *all* estranged from an original homeland. That's what everyone is searching for, no matter how sideways it comes out. We are all *already whole* and trying to find our way Home.

Wow. If all of this was true, then there was nothing to fix. I'd been trying to become someone else for so long that this was revolutionary. Adam and Eve had shown me that the distant memory of that original state of wholeness is what was driving my longing for love—a love that is universal but experienced in the personal. All my striving for love was *really* striving for a restoration of my essential wholeness, something that was—at my core—already true. Groundbreaking! *Now,* I wondered, *how the hell do I find my way Home?*

Several nights later, waking again in the wee hours, another phrase ricocheted: *One must pass through death in order to be transformed.* Again, I lay in bed pondering. *Is this like a dark night of the soul? Is this what Lo and Dave's cancer journey is about? What death must I face in order to be transformed?* I realized that in order to find my way back to a state of wholeness, old habits would need to die—habits that kept me from knowing my true nature. Investigating the patterns, attitudes, and defenses born from an original wound—the archetypal one of existential homelessness *and* the personal ones from within my family of origin—would open doors to my more authentic self. Lo and I were walking distinct but similar paths: Lo through cancer, me through search-ing to know myself, and both of us wanting to experience an ease within. We were enacting an archetypal struggle that is part of being human, each of us walking the transpersonal journey in a personal way, just like the gods and goddesses of mythic stories across all cultures. My relationship with Lois *was* that archetypal struggle, and it was the crucible in which we were learning, grow-ing, and reclaiming the love and wholeness that is our birthright.

Remember

While I was tossing about with realizations in my sleep world, Lois was bridging the worlds of personal wounding and divine love in a different way. She struggled with fears and depression, addressing them by decorating affirmations with colorful and cheerful designs posted all over their house. Phrases like, "I fully breathe in the healing life force—I exhale my fears," "I am strong, calm, and centered," "I am motivated to live a creative life," and, of course, "All that matters is LOVE," helped her reclaim her inner strength. She was reclaiming lost bits and pieces of herself and turned them into a poem called *Remember*—a map for re-membering herself, restoring wholeness as she grappled with feel-ing broken. I let the poem in. I let it move me, posting it on my refrigerator and at my office. I admit I still judged her for some of the practices, like how she took eating consciously to the nth degree, leaving me squirming in my seat, praying to the deities of all the worlds that she'd *finish the meal already!* But all these years later, I still treasure the poem's wisdom and smile as I remember Lo's excitement when she shared it. I share it with you, a reminder of what is essential:

Remember to breathe deeply
Remember to drink lots of water throughout the day
Remember to have positive thoughts
Remember that I am God

Remember to get plenty of exercise
Remember to stay open to the highest and the best
In everything
Remember to see the God in others; that everything is One
Remember to Love myself

Remember to have courage
Remember to keep flexible in body, mind, and spirit
Remember to be joyful and laugh at the littlest things
Remember to do things that feed me most
And do everything for God

Remember to spend time outside
Remember to be gentle with myself
Remember to nourish my body with healthy foods and
Remember to eat consciously and slowly

Remember to read uplifting material
Remember to let go of all resistance—overt and subtle

Remember to live in the present moment
Remember to Just Do It!

Remember to feel the blessing of each new day
Remember to find play in everything I do
Remember to do spiritual practices—
Yoga, meditate, study, chant God's name, selfless service

Remember to keep good company and
Stay in contact with friends
Remember to approach life with wonder and amazement
Remember that it's all perfect!

Remember to stay in the witness state—
That I am not the doer
Remember that all things happen for a reason

Remember to trust my Heart

—Lois Joy Myers

God? The Voice of the Skeptic

"Remember that I am God." "See the God in others." "Do it all for God." The word God is made of just three little letters…what a small word for such a vast energy. God was part of our search for wholeness—both Lois's and mine—though I tended to use different language. God is *not* a four-letter word, but it might as well be for all the misunderstandings and wars that have been waged over it. When I use the word God, it's not about a deity or a person on a throne in the sky passing judgment at the pearly gates. Instead, God translates into *Indescribable Mystery*—words for the mysterious animating force in all things. I recently learned that a new scientific discovery, the Boson-Higgs particle, has been named the God Particle. It is found in all matter. Like DNA, the God Particle is invisible to the naked eye but tangible to those who have the equipment to see it. I think the God Particle is what I experienced while camping when I was nineteen, young, wild, and free. I was cuddled like a puppy with friends in a beanbag chair and surrounded by crisp, cold air and the scent of wood smoke wafting from nearby campfires. The noisy, beer-drinking party of my college compatriots fell away, and I fell into a deep reverie as I gazed into a night sky of infinite stars. Looking into that immeasurable darkness, alive with pinpoints of light—a million suns, each with their own infinite galaxies—was a watershed moment for me. Infinity, somehow close and intimate, invoked such a state of wonder that I felt at once tiny and insignificant in the vastness, yet important—a being with purpose. I was acutely aware that, along with the stars, the purple wildflowers, and the mossy forest in which I lay, *I* had been created. Me, Lily. I was part of the whole—a piece of the entire puzzle of reality made of all people, plants, animals, earth, and everything that existed in the cosmos. I knew in the heart of my soul, in an instant, that everything is connected. Before science named it, I'd experienced the God Particle and realized that everything in all the vastness of the universe had purpose. My desire to know mine was born in that second. The boundaries of what I'd known to be real were stretched beyond comprehension, and my belief in something larger than physical reality became as tangible as the shoes on my feet.

Yet in my patriarchal lineage of persecution, God is rejected. I sometimes feel my dad and his sister standing on either shoulder, whispering into my ears that it's all hocus-pocus. They nearly stop me from writing the word God. My dad would rage, "There is no God!" followed by, "Any God who would let the Holocaust happen is no God I would worship!" Having heard his litany many times, I imagine how impotent he must have felt on a ship in the South Pacific, protecting the religious freedom his father sought in fleeing his homeland. Facing the slaughter of millions of Jews must have exacted such a deep gash in my father that, in the face of his peoples' suffering, he could not—would not—turn to God. Ironically, he wasn't able to see the paradox of being angry at something he proclaimed didn't exist, so his existential pain went unmet. I felt the deepest compassion for him, secretly thinking *he must believe in God because, otherwise, what is he raging against?* My father taught me of the presence of Some Thing because I knew that his anger and hurt were being directed Some Where.

My Aunt Elaine, like brother-like sister, is a staunch atheist who also proclaims at the dinner table, "When you die, you die. That's it. There is nothing more than this physical world." Oddly, we have often fallen into discussion about God. It was Elaine who took me and my cousin, Sophia, to the ocean during the late 1950's. We stayed in 'San Sou-cei' a tiny blue cottage nestled into the dunes just north of Ocean City, Maryland. Each day Sophia and I finagled our way out the bedroom window in the early morning dew while Elaine slept, oblivious. Once free, we wound trails through the tall grasses and bulrushes on the dunes. In my memory, all of it is infused with light – the water, the shells, the sand, even the toads we caught and kept in sand buckets as pets. Once awake, Aunt Elaine made our lunches to take to the beach. And every day she'd call us away from the cold water's edge, wrap our little bodies in towels and take off the wet bathing suits beneath. She'd sit us down, secretly naked, soaking in the warm sun as we ate our baloney and mustard sandwiches. The sun's warmth and love expressed in this sensuous way is cast deeply in me, divinity wrapped up in a towel.

In spite of her disbelief, Elaine helped shape my faith in the sun's invisible warmth and light that is the source of all life. Because the beauty of nature is how I connect with God; it's what many indigenous people call the *Great Mystery*. The wild world carries that mystery right into my soul, and earth becomes my holy temple, where I give praise to the sacred. However it appears—a tiny tree pushing itself through a crack in the sidewalk, a verdant valley of grapevines, a red-rock canyon carved by ancient waters, or a grove of the mighty redwood—these are my definitions of God.

Seer

Around the time Lois and I had begun truth talking and she'd turned her cancer journey into a path with the principle that *love is all that matters*, I'd gone to a ten-day workshop called Seer, modeled on indigenous initiatory rites translated for the modern, western mind, including three days of silence and fasting. It was held on Maui at the edge of a mossy, damp rainforest bordered by a banana grove. As I entered my room, I was greeted by the wafting scent of plumeria blossoms strung into a lei, beauty melting tension from my mind and knots from my shoulders. Seer was designed to initiate the *third eye,* the seat of intuition and gateway to the cosmos, to reveal how spirit manifests on earth. By opening second sight, we'd be able to see the fabric of existence that lies behind the curtain of ordinary reality, but also, just as importantly, we'd see truths about ourselves within that larger context. Though daunting, the insights promised to be healing. I was not disappointed. Three life-changing revelations arrived while I was resting under the Maui sun.

On one of the early days of the retreat, the leader shared an idea that rang bells in my body. "For those of you who, along with your siblings, have not or will not have children, it is the ending of your line. Your entire ancestral lineage, your clan-wave, is coming into completion of its full purpose for existence." Little hairs stood up on top of the goose bumps on my arms. *Sally, Lois, and I are ending our clan-wave.* The long matriarchal and patriarchal lines of my mother and father—our entire ancestry all the way back before names and places—were being carried by the three of us for some as yet to be understood purpose. I prayed that we three would have the clarity and courage to carry our mission to completion.

During the fast, I had an awake-but-dreamlike vision and a sleeping dream; both of which touched me deeply. The vision revealed that I was not the victim of Lois's criticism; it was the opposite. I watched the scene unfold in my mind as I stabbed her with a huge spear through her heart. She lay bleeding on the floor while I flourished. In the sky, like a sun shining down on us, was an image of my father, the light bulb around which our lives revolved. His lineage may have been the source of the dynamic dance between Lo and me, just as the sun was the source of all life. I'd been unconsciously bowing to God, my father—or maybe it was God, *The Father*—my whole life. I think it was both. I had succumbed, in a personal way, to his nature, making myself in his image, driving my life from within his chariot. Lois had, too; she had bowed to the God of Accomplishment so that we aimed our spears at one another in an archetypal battle. We were carrying out the sins of our fathers' fathers all the way back through time. By "sins," I mean errors against one's soul. As we waged against one another, Lois and I sinned against our own souls, perhaps in an attempt to right wrongs—ancestral battles from before we were born. But no matter the cause, the pain to our own hearts ran deep. I didn't have words for this ancestral perspective back then, but I did have the will to start owning up to my violence as a contribution to our conflicts. I began realizing that my reality was flawed. The harsh words with which I'd stabbed her, words like, "I hated..." and, "I can't," and, "I'm not your friend anymore," may have felt true in the moment, but they were not true in the deepest sense of our sisterhood. I was humbled as I wondered whether Lo and I were carrying out something for our whole clan, but mostly I felt remorse as I witnessed the violence I'd waged against her.

The sleeping dream, which followed the vision, opened a whole new layer to our dance. In it, Sally, Lois, and I were on a toboggan-like sled at the top of a pristine, snow-covered mountain range—perhaps the Himalayas. Everything was blinding and radiant, like jewels reflecting the sun. The shimmering beauty overtook us. We float-sailed down the mountains in unified sync with one another, one force embodied as three. As soon as I woke, I scurried to the art supplies, wanting to capture the image on paper, glitter-white-diamonds on white, trying to express the divinity of the mountain peaks and the sensation of the three of us as one being—smooth as silk in glimmering spirit bodies, flying-sledding several feet off the ground. Not until years later did I notice that Lois and I had shared the same symbol of the divine in our dreamtime—Himalayan snow-covered peaks.

Even with truth telling and my decision to trust her, I never shared with Lois the vision in which I'd stabbed her through the heart. I told Sally and myself it was because she was too fragile, and I didn't want to inflame the embers of our always-at-the-ready fires. But I think it was really shame that kept me mute—shame at my own violence, which I struggled to accept. I did adopt new attitudes and behaviors with her, each one a practice of growing stronger in love. I stopped myself from aiming darts. When I felt victimized, I talked it through—sometimes with Lo, sometimes with Sal, Seth, or a friend. With big sighs, I started letting go of the certainty that I was right, putting my sword back into its sheath and bowing to the altar of compassion instead. The twists and turns of our roller-coaster relationship didn't level out completely. But the ride, like our smooth sail down the mountain, got a lot less bumpy.

Five

Practice, Practice, Practice

That first night I got the breast cancer diagnosis, Dave and I both cried about having to go through this AGAIN! I sped through all the emotions that I had never gone through with the other cancers, including anger and doubt, questioning my faith.

I'd been praying for the highest and best, so as I thought about having cancer again and again, I realized that it is really a-GAIN and a-GAIN. Since I no longer believe in the words good or bad, I'm seeing this third cancer as a GAIN, realizing that, in essence, this cancer IS the best way to get me to wherever I'm headed.

This is very freeing. I want to practice remembering this decision in every moment of every day. Eventually I hope it will come naturally.

—Lois

The Triumvirate

Lois and Dave were in their cancer-free phase when it came time to move M&M out of the Carla Road house in Northwest Baltimore—a home in the heart of their original community, the place where they'd grown up, met, married, and eventually re-rooted in retirement. Once restored to their homeland, they had futzed in the garden, wandered through garage sales, eaten silver queen corn with juicy garden tomatoes on the screened porch, and hosted couples from high school with the grace and ease of skilled restaurateurs. But now the refrigerator was dirty, the milk often sour, and weeds grew in the gardens. Parkinson's and Alzheimer's ousted Mason and Margie from their home, demanding the support of assisted living. And they needed their girls to do the down-sizing. We three rode in on our white horses, wrangling a lifetime of stuff, only to discover that the move was just the beginning. We would need to parent M&M in every other way, too. After a call from Jewish Family Services alerted us to numerous unpaid bills, we found the checkbook in complete disarray. The time had come to dig through file cabinets and desk drawers for keys and combinations, long-term care and health-insurance policies, investment plans, Medicare explanation of benefits, social-security cards, driver's licenses, lists of doctors (at least five apiece), medications, VA accounts, bank statements, safe-deposit box contracts, and more—the myriad logistics of living a life. It was a mess—as messy as the insides of their deteriorating brains. Sad and disheartened, we were amazed that they'd held it together at all. They'd been hiding the formidable disarray from us but also, I think, from themselves. The longer they could hold onto their parental roles, the easier it was to avoid facing their growing frailties.

We three sisters met in Sally's cozy living room, Lo and I on the deep-purple love seat wrapped in one of Mom's hand-knit afghans, with light streaming through stained glass in the bay window. We set about planning the move and how we would care for M&M in their new lives. We put newsprint pads on easels and made lists in colored markers. Then we outlined tasks in rainbow hues hung on the mantle, the walls, and in doorways, sipping sweetly scented teas (and later, wine) until everything had been poured out onto the paper, our heads emptied of information. Eventually we figured it out, categorizing tasks and logistics. We took on our first assignments: Lois was the insurance manager, Sally the medical maven, and me, chief of finances.

Keeping up with the sorting process had been especially hard for Lo, and she grew frustrated. With the pressure of time, giving Lo enough space to gather her wits and words was hard for Sal and me, too. All three of us needed to say our piece, even if it had already been said, which was very time consuming. Lois would burst out with an angry accusation, "You aren't listening to me!" or, "You have to respect M&M's ability to make that decision!" I struggled to set aside passive-aggressive sighs or defensive retorts. Slow, deep breaths helped me to remember that I loved my sister, that her blunt words came from her scarred frontal lobe, and that I *wanted* her input. I practiced acting with respect, remembering that I had sheathed my sword. So when she suggested that we stop puzzling M&M's lives together for a moment to each pull an Angel card in a small ceremony, I complied, albeit with an inner eye roll.

Angel cards each carry a single word or phrase for a positive human trait. The words we each pulled were so uncannily perfect for us that I actually surrendered to those Angel cards—a triangle of words for the triad of us. Something in me gave way, and I offered my whole heart to the three of us when we pulled out fresh newsprint and, with our colored markers, drew a triangle—a sacred pact made concrete on the page—as an image of our commitment to parent our parents together. The day had begun in duty but ended as a spiritual path. We were walking the trail hand in hand. The light in the room seemed to brighten as we wrote the Angel card words: Lois, *devotion* and *sacred duty;* Sally, *gratitude* and *perfection;* Lily, *vigilance* and *faith.* Words to live by and qualities to practice. The glow of the setting sun softened the edges in the room and in us as we faced our parents' mortality.

I shared my realization from Seer—that we are the final burst of our ancestral potency, the end of our clan-wave. And I described my Himalayan dream, the three of us slip-sailing through the snow with the sense of oneness that felt like spiritual union. We didn't need a lot of words after that. Our pact became a vow as sure as any taken between people, a triad of partnership in service to our parents, to our clan line, and in spiritual service to life.

Meanwhile, back on planet earth, we returned our attention to the tangible planning, afraid that M&M would resist our decision in their desire to remain independent. Once the triad was fully aligned, it was impossible *not* to surrender. When we met with M&M and laid our love on the table, they surprised us with gratitude, relieved and proud that their daughters would come together in solidarity and devotion to them. That is when Sally, Lois, and

I realized the power of our alignment, the power of three working together as one, just as the dream had revealed. With a triangle of love spread between Oakland, Austin, and Baltimore, we discovered that once we set our minds toward something, it would manifest. This is how we earned, by blood and love, the name Dave eventually gave us: *The Triumvirate.*

The Triumvirate

When it came to the actual packing, sorting, and moving, Lois and I added our flavors to the Baltimore Myers stew, sometimes delicious and smooth, sometimes red-hot and fiery. Lois demanded we slow down and listen to Mom's every story about every item. She protected M&M's autonomy at all costs. I was passionate about completing tasks and stayed focused on the looming deadline. We argued over how to make decisions while haggling over what to do with this tablecloth or that silver service. Neither of us cared much about the items for ourselves; it was more that they were a screen onto which we projected our losses. Loss of our parents as we'd known them. Loss of Lois's natural capacities. Loss of our family home, which held so many memories. While we worked our way through the mire, Dad and Mom bickered and picked at each other over who was or wasn't doing what, which often descended into loud quarreling, both of them angry and scared until, eventually, Mom would cry, and they'd go into their separate corners. *Who were these people?* It was chaotic, not to mention completely uncharacteristic of them. *Strangers are inhabiting my parents' bodies!* It was agony to watch my normally calm, collected, and organized mother unable to keep a simple decision clear in her mind and my efficient, tidy and functional father unable to pack a single box. We were referees, calming and comforting them, even as our own inner children needed to be held. Though excruciating, we had no choice but to sit in the stew and simmer until the dining room was stacked full of boxes. Dealing with so much loss aged us, honed us, and matured us.

I took on the role that Dad had vacated, going with the cut-off-and-just-do-it approach—making decisions, moving like lightening, putting everything in order. Lois took Mom's more feeling role, cajoling with, "Let's take our time," Or, "Let *them* decide, Lil!" But I would forge ahead, making what I thought of as executive decisions, taking boxes to Goodwill, or trash bags to the curb late at night to keep my Depression-era dad from foraging for trinkets he might need one day or doodads he simply couldn't live without. Sally, the local sister in charge of the whole *megillah* (a Yiddish version of the expression, *the whole nine yards*), showed up with dinners and practicalities of square footage and moving dates. Little by little, we packed, sold, gave away, shipped, or stored a lifetime of dishes, furniture, honey-do tools, photo albums, and collectibles. Nearly sixty years of life was reduced to an assisted-living apartment at The Atrium. Our family home and our parents, both nests of safety, were dismantled. As M&M lost their sanity, along with their beloved home and garden, grief followed us through the house. To our credit, we handled ourselves with something akin to right action, never reaching the boiling point. We practiced respect. We listened to one another, even when we disagreed. We managed to appreciate each other's strengths and let the weaknesses slide. It dawned on us that our different approaches were complementary, like colors of the rainbow. As we expanded our palettes, we discovered that, when it came to parenting M&M, one color did the trick as well as any other.

Lois and I overlapped our trips by a few days when we could, but more often, we were ships passing in the night, holding metaphorical hands with one another on cell phones as pressures rained down on our heads. We tracked each other's travel schedules, as Sally held the home fort together, one of us always on call to be there for the ranting, weeping, laughing, or abundant comedic and tragic descriptions of the craziness my parents' lives had fallen into. Many a time I sat at the airport awaiting a flight home to Oakland—these were fertile moments for feelings to burst forth—crying to Sal or Lo on my cell. Miraculously, eight trips later, we shoehorned M&M out of their house and into the Atrium apartment, breathing a huge, collective sigh of relief.

Oy! Is Just One Part of Joy

About a year later, breast cancer strode into our lives. Lois and I had begun a sweeter, softer, cautious but honest cycle of love. She had been called in for a biopsy after an irregular mammogram, and then sent a confidential e-mail to Sally and me, not yet wanting to share the news with extended family or community. It was titled, "Oy! Oy! Oy!" I pictured her angular body dancing to the music she and Dave put on to "release, release, release." I imagined her sharp arms and shoulders, elbows, knees, and feet moving as I read that her "cells were full of light, jumpin' and dancin' and laughin'." She became certain it would turn out to be nothing. While Lo danced, Sally and I held our breath until the biopsy came back, gasping when we heard the news. Malignant. *You have to be kidding me!* For the third time in ten years, Lois had cancer—not a metastasis of the brain cancer but a completely different strain—the rarity of it sending electric shocks all the way down to my toes. I had to suspend disbelief, which I would have preferred to wrap around myself like a blanket. When the small lump in one breast led to a discovery of a second one in the other, she went through countless tests to learn about everything from estrogen levels to her genetic predisposition for breast cancer as an *Ashkenazi* Jew. The whole thing was unbelievable. Though Lo's long-ago dream of sinking into quicksand had shown me what was coming, I was anything but prepared for this spiral down into the mud.

Dancing herself from anger to surrender, and with Dave's clear-minded support, Lois settled into the firm belief that this cancer would not define her. She became a spiritual witness to all that was happening to her. I was impressed with how much she'd grown, no longer the fearful girl who first got on that gurney for brain surgery ten years before. Now a strong and courageous woman, she needed hands to hold, but she didn't need coddling. And that was huge maturation—a transformation from fear to love. I was, once again, proud of my Big Sister. She'd gotten damn tired of being at the center of the cancer storm, so she became the engineer of her own life, determining exactly how she would go through it. Lois thought long and hard about how each treatment would impact her quality of life, then armed with information about risks, rates of survival, side effects, and options she called me and asked, "What do you think? If it were you, what would you choose?" I wasn't the only one she asked, but I felt the pressure of wanting to help, to give the right answer. Reaching down deep, I remembered her dream—both the quicksand and the blue pearl. Recalling what I'd known then, that Lo would have a long, difficult journey through cancer and that it would ultimately take her life, I found the words, "I'd opt for quality over quantity. Focus on living now, being present to the life in front of you." *No more suffering from medical treatments! With a low-percentage possibility of cure, it's not worth it,* I thought, but did not say. She made her own decision to skip the full mastectomy in favor of the lumpectomy. She surrendered to the cancer as her "best and highest good, since that's what Life is giving me" and moved forward with an upbeat approach. Lois zoomed through surgery and kept both of her beautiful breasts, even as lymph nodes were removed. She received radiation and took oral chemo, which tired her but was not debilitating. When she decided to let a portion of her community know about the new cancer, Dave was right there beside her, running interference, staunching the well-intentioned but often undermining advice that just about everyone felt entitled to offer. A friend of theirs pressured them to move out of their house, certain of toxicity as the cause of their cancers. That was not necessary, though only a small victory in the overall scheme of things. Lo and Dave had quietly done their homework, testing the soils around their house, finding no toxins. With a truly restored respect for my sister, I responded to their friend, "Lois and Dave know the risks and rewards well enough to make their own decisions. I trust that they are living whatever life or soul-contract they came here to live. Whether or not it makes sense to us, we need to trust them to make their own journey in their own way." She listened, then agreed to take a step back, saying, "I just wish they didn't have to suffer like this." Joining her in vulnerability, I softly responded, "Me, too."

Dave sent a strident but necessary e-mail reminding their community that their lives were about much more than cancer, saying, "We can do without pity or directives about what we need to do." He clarified further with, "We want to share the Light with you all, the Joy of existence, and the Love in our hearts, trusting that Spirit will take care of the true healing." I found his words comforting. It restored my own belief that, while Lois might not be cured, healing would be a different matter entirely. Dave's faith in the invisible world awakened my deepening respect, especially because I knew it wasn't a *la-la-love and light* thing; it was grounded in real life and his own grappling with challenged faith. He'd had an unexpected but direct encounter with his father's spirit one evening as he unloaded groceries from the car. Amid the most mundane of daily tasks, chills ran up his spine as Dave heard his father's voice from behind pronounce the words, "See you soon, Davey. I love you." Scared by the words but profoundly touched by the visitation, Dave's faith deepened. I felt something akin to awe for his attunement to the spiritual realm and for his ever-deepening heart. It wasn't as if he—or they—felt only joy. Of course not! But he held true to the courage of his convictions. They both allowed their suffering to make room for a larger story: Love. I practiced living by their words, inspired by how they moved forward honestly, faced their cancer with heart, and walked a tightrope of hope laced with heavy doses of reality. At first I'd thought that joy was about being positive, but then I recognized that Lois and Dave lived with joy as a form of surrender. Joy, I discovered, came from trusting in life regardless of circumstance. I really got it; Lo showed me that "oy" truly was only one part of joy.

Vigil One - Vigil Two - Vigil Three

We'd just jumped the breast cancer hurdle when The Triumvirate was called to a family meeting by The Atrium. We were told, "In order to keep your father here, he'll need a feeding tube. Otherwise, he'll need to move to a skilled-nursing facility." Pneumonia, caused by a weakened swallowing mechanism, was common in Parkinson's patients and is typically what took their lives. The Atrium was unable—or unwilling—to risk him choking. Dad had just come home from the hospital—antibiotics keeping pneumonia at bay—but it was only a matter of time. *Dad's dying.* "The other option is for him to go into hospice care. Then he can stay here," they told us. *Dad's dying.* With limited choices looming, our hearts churned with sorrow. Hardly prepared for this moment, we huddled in the hallway—a group hug in which to cry and gather strength. *Dad's dying.* Dad, at eighty-six, may have needed to be lifted in and out of bed, but he was still in charge of his destiny. We determined that, from his wheelchair and in spite of his difficulty speaking, this would be *his* choice. We collected ourselves for the sobering rite of passage and gathered in a circle, surrounded by family photos and a lush forest of greenery in the sunny window while Dizzy Gillespie and his Big Band played on the boom box. *Dad's dying.* The moment of truth arrived as Sally laid it out, "Dad, here's the drill. You have two equally bad choices if you are to stay here at The Atrium: a feeding tube or entering hospice care, knowing that the end is near. Otherwise, we'll have to move you into a nursing home." *Good job, Sal, no pussyfooting around, just like Dad would want.* "What do you all think?" he asked. Sally answered first, tearfully, "It's up to you, Dad. I support whatever you decide. I love you." Around the circle, each person repeated this same phrase until my turn. *C'mon, Lily, be brave!* I gathered every bit of courage I had, knowing I had to break through the niceties. "Dad, you've lived a full and amazing life. You had a great, successful business. You've traveled and seen the world. You've raised three beautiful daughters. There is nothing left that you have to do. It's OK for you to go." And after a pause, "It's fine with me if you go." Silence.

Then a whispered, "I agree with Lily," was echoed around the circle one by one. He looked at each of us—mouth hanging open, drool sliding to the bandanna bib he was wearing. "Then it's unanimous," he said. Turning to Mom, looking deep into her, and with the thick musicality of compassion for her pain but in an unusually crystal-clear voice, he said, "Cut me loose, Ma."

He'd made his decision. Slowly, my mother turned her face toward his like she'd done a million times, locking eyes. With lucidity and sorrow, she accepted her husband's determination. "It's hard," was her simple reply. And with that, we let our tears fall, rolling off cheeks and chins. *He's so ready. He's been waiting for this,* I thought, offering private gratitude for the practice of truth telling, which had paid off in that moment. *This is exactly right.* I looked into my father's eyes, and we spoke no words. None were needed. It was a soul-to-soul encounter, during which I realized the depth of his love and how it had shaped me. In one instant, the clearest knowing came over me: even the difficult parts had been infused with his love—his tantrums, his self-absorption, his work-work-work abandonment of me. I saw my father for who he truly was, maybe for the first time. Unconditional love flowed between us like sweet wine. With no words left to speak, Lois turned to Dad and said, "Wanna dance?" We turned up the boom box, Lo circled him in her arms and pulled him from the wheelchair in an embrace. Feet planted solidly, we laughed and cried and held him steady as they danced. Though it was just arms swaying with fingers interlaced, Dad's huge smile for the camera was priceless. It became a moment of celebration, a sacred marriage of joy and sorrow walking hand in hand. The word vigilance, my corner of the triangle, took on new meaning as I came to understand its connection to vigil—a holy time of watchfulness. We'd just finished our first one.

Sally, Lois, Dad, Me, and Mom after the Hospice Decision Dance
Lois and Dad dancing in 1969 (that's me watching them!)

Like Lois, Dad danced in the face of death. This, too, was my ancestral heritage—the ability to dance through sorrow. The man who, hand in hand with his beloved wife, spent a lifetime in dogged pursuit of his goals, who'd built two highly successful restaurants out of his father's cigar store, and raised three strong, independent daughters, determinedly chose hospice with dignity, purpose, and love. With his joyful spirit still shining through his eyes, my dad, Mason I. Myers, turned toward death instead of staying alive just to stay alive. As the days blended, one into the other, The Triumvirate flowed in and out of his room in a second vigil, taking turns visiting and ensuring his comfort. He stayed awake to take pleasure in our company and asked for his favorite food—fresh strawberries—which Sally fed to him in tiny bites. One memorable afternoon, when all three of us were gathered beside his bed, I remembered that though he could barely talk, he was still able to sing. I searched my memory for a song to which we'd all know the words. The Jewish prayer honoring the oneness of all life, the Sh'ma, burst into my head. I started singing, and everyone joined in, with Dad's voice loud and clear. Over and over, we chanted, *"Sh'ma y'srael, adonai elohenu adonai echaud,"* meaning *"Hear, O Israel; the Lord our God, The Lord is One."* Those were his last words. The proclaimed atheist celebrated words of oneness and spirit, and then, as if he were complete, he dropped into a deep quiet. He'd turned inward to begin his passage toward whatever lay beyond this world. That was the beginning of the third vigil.

During his final hours, the three of us had been meditating, knowing he was ready to pass at any moment. He lingered. We wondered how to help him go, and we told him, "Dad, you did a great job. We're fine, and Mom will be fine. We'll take care of her. You're going to live on, through us. It's OK to go." After a long silence, I said, "We'll walk alongside you to the edge of the cliff, but we can't go over it with you." Lois added, "Maybe you want to dance over it?" Almost imperceptibly, his toes wiggled. And still he held on. *What was holding him back?* Sally signaled for us to leave him. Once in the other room, she whispered, "We're in his way. He's hanging on to be with us." That's when we realized he needed privacy and agreed to only enter Dad's room to ensure comfort, moving one at a time, soundlessly in and out of the sanctuary. We also took turns being with Mom, who lay in the other room on the double bed they'd shared for sixty years, keeping conversations simple, mostly roundabouts in which she'd immediately forget whatever we'd discussed moments before. She occasionally asked, "Do you think he'll make it?" When we gently reminded her that he was, in fact, dying, she'd respond with, "No, me either." After some quiet reflection, she'd lucidly add, "I think he's going to die." Night came, and it was Sally's turn to sleep with Mom, so Lois and I headed to our Atrium guest apartment with its single, smaller-than-twin-size beds. We brushed our teeth and talked—and talked some more until I said, "Lo, we have to go to sleep now, because you know we're going to get a call tonight!" Just as we finally crawled into those tiny beds, Lois nodding in agreement, the phone rang, and adrenaline shot through me. We heard Sally whisper, "He's gone," and like mirror images of one another, Lo and I leapt into an embrace. I shouted, "Yay, Dad! You did it! Hooray! You did it!" while Lo broke into sobs, our opposite responses erupting from the same place—our hearts. We scrambled, bumping into each other as we grabbed our clothes, then held hands as we took the stairs two at a time on our way to Dad's sanctuary.

Mom had awakened at midnight, claiming she'd heard Dad call her name, then found he'd passed. She and Sal waited for us, hearts shattered open, so the four of us could enter his room together. *He's really gone.* Lois and I stood side by side, and I felt her reach an arm around my shoulders, drawing me close. As I turned, raising my arm in response, I was stunned to see her a foot away, arms at her sides, gazing at Dad's body. She must have felt something, too, because she suddenly turned to look at me, eyes wide. An instant later, the feeling was gone, and I knew that it had been Dad who had squeezed me—maybe us—in a good-bye. Mom crawled into the bed beside his body and stroked this face that we would never lay eyes on again. From some ancient inner knowing, we moved together, preparing his body, bathing it tenderly, then dressing him in his favorite fishing vest over a multicolored shirt tucked into a pair of jeans. We placed one of his fifty-some hats on his head so that this body looked like Mason, not just an old man who'd died in a hospital bed in assisted living.

Mason Myers was a cowboy who loved watching Westerns, identifying with the hero who righted the wrongs in the small claptrap villages of the Wild West, capturing the wily outlaw in a shootout. Despite being a bit of an outlaw himself, he stood up as the do-right man. He loved the swell of orchestral music at the end of these movies, when streams of light poured onto the wide, western vista. He had a name for those visible threads of light through the clouds: God Music. Lois put on a CD of cowboy songs, and we created our own God Music as we sang along with Roy Rogers and Dale Evans: "*Ha-ppy Tra-a-ils to you…until we meet again…Happy tra-a-a-i-ils to you. Keep smilin' un-til then.*" On key, off-key, and through laughter and tears, we sent our dad's spirit off into the Great Beyond.

Let's Do It!

The next day, waves of grief started coming over me unexpectedly. My father was dead. Gone. The four of us took turns bursting into tears, and with Mom like a zombie, Sally, Lois, and I decided how to memorialize him. We divided the tasks before us: calling friends and family, finding a location for the service, ordering food and flowers, and picking up his ashes. We alternated staying with Mom. Dave and Seth arrived (since Don and Sally had recently separated, Don dropped in but did not stay), true brothers in solidarity with each other and in service to their wives. They treasured each other, secretly marveling at the crazy but wonderful Myers clan. They did whatever we asked, from walking Mom up and down Atrium hallways, reminding her that Dad was being cremated, to picking up take-out or going to the crematory to retrieve Dad's ashes. M&M had chosen cremation years before at a small mortuary where Mom had marveled at the tiny urns, laughingly telling us to put a smidgen of her ashes in a cute one after she was gone. But she could remember none of that now, nor imagine her husband's body consumed by fire. Walking up and down the halls soothed her, a well-loved and deeply trusted son-in-law on each arm. When it was my turn to sleep with her, she screamed in a nightmare, fighting me off as if I were the grim reaper coming to get her, too, when I tried to calm her by stroking a shoulder. I finally soothed her, then as she drifted back into sleep I felt terror rising in my throat and churning in my belly. *This is too hard to do alone.* Finally, exhausted from lack of sleep, I called Sally's at first light, waking Seth to say, "I need someone to be with me. Please, come. Now." Later, knees wobbly, I spilled tears over lunch at Applebee's after we'd picked out urns at the crematory. Lois struggled; she had been keeping up, but we could see, from her green-tinged, pale face; she was wearing out. Sally tried to get her to slow down, reminding her to take care of herself, but she would have none of it and got angry when I wrote the obituary without her. She was still taking oral chemo and was just too worn down to help but felt left out. Fighting against surrender, she wanted Sally and I to slow down to her rhythm. I was powerless to meet her need, as if my psyche's volume had been turned up loud, the activity knob of my whole being set to DO. Sally and I were everywhere at once, filling the hole of Dad's dying with busyness. I was channeling all my grief into doing, doing, doing. Lois said, "I feel bad because you're doing stuff, and I'm not." I understood, but all I wanted was for her to stop demanding that I be different so she could feel better. I'm not proud of my impatience, but it was there, and it was real. I felt really sad, too, not just for her but for all three of us, as tension built and made it harder to connect. And God knew, The Triumvirate needed one another right then. Deeply.

I started thinking about how we learned to value doing over being in our family. Dad, especially, was a doer. Though this value system had merit, it also missed some very important aspects of living. When Sally remembered Lo's point on our triangle and her words, *sacred duty* and *devotion,* she said, "I don't think it's true that you aren't doing anything." As Lo's Angel card words, *sacred duty,* shot through me, I reminded her, "*Lo, you are our space holder!* You are the witness to the bigger picture—that's your sacred duty, which *truly* means more than all the *doing* in the world!" I shifted from impatience to inspiration when I invited her to "Just own this role! Surrender to it rather than trying to be something else." With force, but not without compassion, I followed with, "Like it or not, Lo, apparently *doing* is *not* your purpose." As she broke into grateful sobs, she answered, "You're right, Lil. I have forgotten that I AM part of who I am." Sally reminded her how she'd welcomed the cancers with beauty and had let them teach her. I shared how I had begun to value what Lois brought, from the inside, and told her how passionately I wanted her to value it, too. I got vulnerable enough to tell her, "I need that space holding from you, Lo." She was silent for a while before acknowledging that if she kept aspiring to be someone that was no longer possible, she would never realize her calling. With courage, she made a decision to accept her new role and surrender to it. She thanked us and later told me, "Lil, I feel like you really understand." That was especially sweet, because I felt like I did, too.

And so, as a restored Triumvirate, we continued to prepare Dad's memorial. To honor him was to celebrate his quirkiness, his business acumen, and his colorful personality, so we snuck into Mom's apartment at the crack of dawn and filled Sally's Camry, plus two rental cars, with Mason memorabilia. From hats and menus from the Heritage House and Myers Restaurant to photos of Ye Olde English Pub and the Zodiac Lounge, the room was filled with color. At the ceremony, we asked everyone to wear one of his hats for the service and to take it home as a reminder of his spirit. With jaunty caps, derbies, imprinted baseball hats, and knitted wool of all colors on heads, the room came alive, just as he would have wanted, in celebration of him! Lois danced her eulogy to Dad's favorite song, Cole Porter's, *"Birds do it, bees do it, even sentimental fleas do it…Let's do it…Lets fall in love!"* She ceremonially put a red bandanna around her neck to honor the cowboy in him as she danced, glowing. Only Sally and I knew that she was, at that moment, in treatment for cancer. As she moved her body to "Let's Do It"—a song about the urge to merge—I saw her beauty, inside and out, her whole, spirited being. Sitting beside Seth, I leaned into him, and the rigidity in my body melted, my quiet, tender weeping turning into outright sobs. I'm sure everyone thought I was crying over Dad (and I was), but mostly I wept for Lois while she radiated light, oblivious to my realization that loss was the cost of wholehearted love. My chest filled with an excruciating desire for her to live.

Two Eggs in a Nest

Soon after, The Triumvirate parted, carrying the values of our soul pact in our hearts. We'd been together for almost a month—and a nearly conflict-free time at that. With Sally nearby to tend to Mom, Lois headed home to Austin and I, to Oakland and my counseling practice. When I opened the door to my third-floor office, I looked, uncomprehending, at the fallen Buddha statue on the floor, twigs and leaves covering every surface, the room in utter disarray. *Had there been an earthquake?* Then I saw her. A bird. A nest. The corner of my couch had become a safe place for new life. The green couch, where clients told their stories (one client called it the crying couch, the one place she felt free to let tears flow) had become home to a pigeon. Ms. Pigeon sat on the crying couch, eyeing me protectively as she strutted back and forth, nervous. That's when I saw the two eggs she'd so carefully laid and tended. I'd left a window open just a few inches, having expected to return the next day, and that was all it took to invite her into the safe haven.

I believe that the thread of connection between worlds is always present and speaking. But this was beyond any synchronicity I'd experienced to date. Greeted by two eggs on a nest on the first day back to work after my father's death was a clear message. The phrase, *"From death springs new life,"* echoed in my mind. Although I had a client about to arrive onto this scene, I didn't rush Ms. Pigeon. As gently as I could, I gathered her nest onto a file folder and placed it tenderly on the ledge outside the window. It was a touchstone, pointing toward some rebirth of my own, though I had no idea what that could possibly be.

The crying couch with two eggs in a nest

Six

A Year to Surrender

Over these years, Lo and I have talked about the possibility of dying and how that might impact the survivor partner and others. Friends and family have not been part of this conversation; they don't know that we manage this aspect of the cancer experience on a daily basis.

We feel grounded in what we know and believe and are readying ourselves for this new level of challenge. We will shed some tears in this journey and don't want others to feel compelled to hide theirs from us. Any show of emotion is a thing of beauty to us and helps us be open about our feelings as well.

—Dave

Camp

With the image of two eggs on a nest urging me onward, I scribbled an intention on a bit of scrap paper—*a job serving nature*—and stuffed it into a clay box that served as my altar. Because Sally gave it to me, and with its triangular nature, I thought of it as my *Triumvirate Power Box.* Just one week later, I was attending a Camps in Common board meeting. Affectionately called CIC, it is the nonprofit operator of Oakland Feather River Family Camp. I'd been on the board ever since I'd volunteered as a summer counselor at the youth camp three years prior. Camp is in my DNA. Besides the fact that our summer vacations at the Magothy were much like the California phenomenon of family camp, my Great Aunt Myrtle owned a day camp where, as a teen, I'd spent summers as a counselor and teen program director. Besides, my parents had met as camp counselors when Mason laid his handkerchief down so Margie wouldn't have to sit on the wet grass.

With its towering ponderosa pines along icy-cold Spanish Creek, Feather River Camp was a place where kids ran free and imaginations soared, where parents sank into easy chairs and played cards alongside the rushing creek, soaking in mountain air as days stretched into forever. But this camp was a sinking ship; the current director had worked herself into exhaustion, and we were deep in fiscal red, with a fed-up bookkeeper and vendors springing out of the woodwork, waving invoices and demanding payment. We were about to declare bankruptcy when I thought, *Caution, be damned!* A volcano erupted in my belly, and my hand, as if it had a mind of its own, shot into the air. Shocked faces turned toward me as words tumbled from my mouth, "I...I...I'll step in!" The rest of the board cheered when I agreed to work for free until we were back in the black, and, just like that, I moved from president of the board to executive director of the small nonprofit that needed serious help if it was to survive. I committed to pull the ship from its hole and turn it around, which was formidable, scary, and overwhelming. Nonetheless, I was off and running, calling on Dad's energy as I sifted, sorted, and rallied the longtime camper troops to collaborate on the tasks ahead. I was stunned that, within one week, my prayer had manifested.

Since Camps in Common was new and Feather River Camp was old, with decades of deferred maintenance, there was an immensity of tasks. Every day brought a new challenge, from broken water treatment and septic systems to equipment failures, punctuated with emergencies. "We're out of water!" "There's a rattlesnake in the lower restrooms!" "Staff are fighting in the kitchen, and the first cook wants to quit!" "We just caught the teen counselors drinking!" Meeting the insatiable needs of camp demanded that I release my private counseling practice. The crying couch now hosted stacks of marketing materials and a flurry of camp interviewees instead of soul seekers. I surrendered the role of soul coach, a loss piggybacked onto losing my dad, and adopted the compelling dynamics of director. I was the hero, saving the day as I fixed the broken bookkeeping, instituted new systems, and cleaned out years of camp debris. I found ample opportunities to make the exquisite five-hour canyon drive to and from camp. Seth joined me a couple times at the beginning, and we walked along Spanish Creek as we held counsel on everything nonprofit—from staff management to fund-raising, he transmitted his extensive knowledge. But slowly, he grew tired of conversations about camp. More and more often I drove alone, singing along to tunes from the 1940s playlist I'd made for Mason's memorial, entitled, *Dad.* As I glanced at the rushing river and wound along the curvy road into the low Sierra mountains, memories of the Magothy and family road trips along Rocky Mountain creeks stirred. It was near to heaven, and I became a *doing* machine—my dad's natural state of being. Along with a daily invocation—*C'mon, help me out, Dad*—I brought my whole heart to the role. Stepping into the shoes of my predecessor, I picked up the weight of the eighty-plus-year-old institution, along with the expectations of generations of Oakland families. Each had their distinct opinion of what would make camp better: "The food is great!" "The food sucks!" "We need more staff!" "We have to cut back on staff!" "We need better staff!" "Bring back singing in the Chow Palace!" "We hate the singing in the Chow Palace!" My head spun, and though I'd heard the adage, "You can't please everyone," I tried. I fielded the input and tried to blend new sensibilities with traditional preferences. My childhood training of surrendering my personal needs to a larger vision was like wearing a comfortable old shoe, though in this case, the shoes were pretty damn big.

I channeled my grief into every moment of every day, making the quirky mountain town of Quincy my camp home for the summer. Seth came for visits during the four months I was away from home, though he found them unsatisfying. Much like my father's jumping-jack routine at the Heritage House dinner table, I was often there-then-gone, called to mitigate some issue in the camp office, store or kitchen. Seth was unhappy living alone in Oakland and found his visits frustrating, but he supported me in my passion, hoping that I'd soon settle into my new role, then turn my attention back to him. As I slowly turned that ship around I was alternately burdened, overwhelmed, and honored to steward the sixty-five acres of land and act as caretaker for the people of Feather River Camp. Before Dad died, Lois confessed that one of her nicknames for me was "Little Daddy." She added, "I hope you don't take that the wrong way," to which I grinned in agreement.

It was fitting; he was a force of nature when it came to manifesting his creative spark, and so was I. When he died, it was natural that I'd pick up his role in our family system, and that came in pretty handy for running camp. *Little Daddy, indeed!* I thought as I adopted my father's free-floating creativity and chutzpah.

Memorial Day Number Three

Lois also had camp in her blood, and I invited her to come for a week as our environmentalist in residence. She'd created a nature-immersion curriculum for Camp Ranchito!, a place for urban youth in Austin, Texas to learn about the outdoors. I was excited for Feather River Camp kids and families to have a taste of Lo. And I was looking forward to sharing my world with her in the magnificent Sierra. On Memorial Day, the annual CIC work weekend, after saying good-bye to Seth (who'd spaciously celebrated our wedding anniversary with me amid sixty-some volunteers), I nestled in my cozy knotty-pine cabin to catch up on voice mails. Lois's strident voice killed the buzz. "Call me back as soon as you can." When she picked up, I cut to the chase, "What happened?" Her blunt answer, "We both have cancer again…we were diagnosed with recurrences *on the same day.*" I stared at the ponderosa pines outside my window, not really seeing them. She kept talking, and I tried to absorb her words until she noticed my silence. "Are you crying?" she asked. "Yes," was my whispered response. Every wired pore of my skin wanted her to be alive and healthy and vigorous. Her trip to camp, and so much more, was not to be. *Both of them? At the same time?* Lois sounded almost excited when she talked about how this was their destiny playing out—how this same-day event reinforced her belief that there was some greater purpose to the cancer than we could possibly know. I got goose bumps when she told me they'd seen a "Thelma and Louise Live!" bumper sticker on the car in front of them as they drove home from the hospital. Thelma and Louise were two characters (in a movie of the same name), who'd chosen the moment of their deaths by ceremoniously driving their top-down Cadillac off the edge of a cliff. When Lois said, "Maybe we'll go out together like they did," Dave answered with wry humor, "There are issues with that...not the least of which is, we don't own a convertible!" But the bumper sticker reinforced her passionate belief that she and Dave would choose their own form and timing for their lives and deaths. As if another brick was laid in her spiritual foundation, she surrendered to the news with an ease I'd not seen in her before.

I wept through the entire conversation, but Lo's spirit was strong. She was steady as a jetty among waves when she described the conversation she and Dave had the night they were diagnosed. Intending to write a book about their cancer journey, she'd said to Dave, "This is quite a story we've got here...this double cancer story." His response is what blew me away, though, "To me it's a double love story. We're shortchanging it to say it's just about cancer. There's so much more to it than that. Other people would see six cancers over eleven years between two people, but *that*, to me, is not the story. It's not about the physical hardships; it's about all the growth and changes that have come with it." They agreed that they were doing life, not cancer, and promised to remind each other that while trying to beat the cancers would be important, the enjoyment of life—the _zest_ of life, the part that makes life worth living—would not be put on hold. In spite of whatever losses cancer would exact, they would "just do things that make us feel alive, whatever that is, in any given time." Intellectually, I supported their philosophy, but in that moment, all I felt was sorrow. When we hung up, I could do nothing but sit in my chair, sobbing until I'd wrung out every last tear. Then I crawled into bed and shoved my head under the pillow.

Service and Surrender

Like father like daughter, I threw myself into camp, *doing* without attention to the costs to my personal life, Seth included. Overwhelmed and completely absorbed for three months, I gave scant attention to Lois and Dave. They surrendered to doing the drill of cancer—fighting for their lives with trademark positivity and dedication. *Besides,* I told myself, *they are in some great hands,* thinking about the amazing outpouring of community support that had led to the birth of The Angels. Their friend and neighbor, Kathy Metzler, who Lois dubbed the Over-Arching Angel, formed the group. The Angels coordinated all things Lois and Dave. From scheduling food prep (meeting their unique, macrobiotic-like diets) and thrice-weekly deliveries to setting up housekeeping and yard work, Kathy made it easy for Lois and Dave to fall into the supportive arms of those who wanted to serve. Lo and Dave felt they "were surrounded by guardian Angels, truly blessed with the richness of friendship," while I marveled at how so *many* people wanted to serve them. One of the Angels told me that she loved supporting

Dave and Lois, often returning home feeling as if she'd had a mini-vacation. Another Angel, an exquisite healer and massage therapist, never asked for anything in return but often cooked all day, bringing exotic vegetarian feasts, along with her magical hands. Their friend Monica's black beans became legendary at the Myers-Akard household. If Dave's tennis buddy and colleague, Rob, was at the door with sautéed greens (one batch cooked extra soft for Dave's sensitive digestion, the second, al dente for Lo), then it had to be Saturday. Jill, from across the street, mowed the lawn and carted trash cans every week, and her husband, Bobby, played honey-do, fixing this and that as needed. Charles, the Over-Arching Angel's husband, tended to Lo's organic vegetable garden, which she was too tired to handle on her own. Someone they didn't even know climbed a tree in the back yard to cut away the dead limbs. It went on and on…and the Over-Arching Angel herself was, well, simply available for anything from insurance snafus to dish-washing, and from taxi-service to vacuuming. If Dave or Lois could think of it, and often when they didn't, Over-Arching Angel, Kathy, was there. From afar, I listened to stories of love in action from Lois and Dave's world and was staggeringly, astoundingly inspired.

Celebration and the Big Scoop

As before, Lo had surgery right away so that, in late spring, she had her third brain tumor removed, just like she was fallin' off a log. Afterward, she said, "From all my spiritual study over these many years, I was able to feel peaceful—a detached witness to everything." Dave told us, "As she came out of anesthesia, she was talking through her oxygen mask, directing the nurses about her meds—in charge of her own ship already!" Since the tumor had morphed into a new, faster-growing strain from the past two, the surgeon planted five Gliadel Wafers in the bed of the tumor to deliver a direct hit of chemo, with no side effects at all. *YAY! You get those bugger-fucking cells!* I thought, assuming that they would keep the cancer at bay for at least another five years as each surgery had done before. Lo was so easy breezy with the whole experience that I felt freed from concerns, turning my focus onto my own ship while she sailed hers. My first summer of camp ended with tremendous accolades as we moved from fiscal red to black, I got paid, and Lois's recovery sped along.

Meanwhile, Dave had a tougher row to hoe. He needed radiation and chemotherapy to reduce the size of his pelvic tumor before surgery was even a viable option, lest he become paralyzed. In his uplifting way, he drew from Gurumayi, of the Siddha Yoga path, when he wrote to us saying, "Our teacher tells us that we're given problems that we're equal to, not larger than or smaller than us, but *equal to*. There's no point in asking why this is happening. Important thing is to know that we're given what we need in every situation." As Angels drove Dave to and from MD Anderson in Houston, others shuttled Lo on errands or to radiation in Austin, staying overnight to ensure her well-being. In Houston, friends offered a furnished apartment within easy walking distance to the medical center—fulfilling Dave's prophecy that he'd receive all he needed. Dave's faith went beyond a positive attitude, even when his chemo treatments went on and on and on for over a year. With each new chemo cocktail, he found capacity to surrender, saying, "We realize that we have no control here and just need to step out of the way so that we can allow the Divine Wisdom to show the way. There's no reason to hang on to what we think this life should be but, rather, be a witness to what is unfolding in order to join in the flow of this magnificent universe." More than an abstract concept for him, Dave lived this principle when the challenges would have gotten the best of most of us. When the influx of toxicity in his body created nearly unbearable side effects, he struggled to focus on what brought joy into his life. When the necrosis (dying cells within his tissues) made it hard to walk and he had to use oven mitts to reach into the refrigerator, his irritability quotient went WAY up. He trudged on, and Lois surrendered her own willfulness when he snapped or sniped unnecessarily.

Yet, when Sally came to California to celebrate her sixtieth birthday, Dave would have it no other way but to join us, side effects be damned! Originally intended to be a meet up in sunny Palm Springs, we moved it to Guerneville when Seth could neither fly nor cross a tall mountain range lest increased air pressure disrupt his restored eyesight from recent emergency surgery for a detached retina. As if his own health wasn't challenged, Dave focused on Seth, checking often on his well-being. After a long day of travel, Lo and I planned Sally's birthday surprise when we found a little dish at a local thrift shop matching Sal's childhood mug with bunnies at the bottom. We giggled as we exclaimed, "Never too late to celebrate the magical inner child!" Later that evening, Lois and Dave radiated happiness at the dinner table. Dave told jokes throughout dinner, pursing and pinching his burning lips to protect them from cracking and bleeding whenever he laughed. *Laughing to keep from crying,* I thought. All weekend I watched Dave alternate between glowing with joy and suffering with discomfort, but mostly I saw him do as he intended, flowing with the magnificent universe in Anderson Woods (one of the few remaining first-growth redwood forests) or at Goat Rock, where the Russian River flows into the ocean. Sally, Lois, and I held an impromptu ceremony at the mouth of the Russian River, tossing Dad's ashes into the air and water with a colony of frolicking harbor seals darting in and out of the powerful currents. A flock of gulls soared, circling over our heads as we released Dad's ashes and bones into the oceanic womb. We passed a bottle of wine in a toast to Mason's life and then tucked ourselves against the cliff, watching the sunset over the ocean. I watched Dave, too, seeing that he soaked up the healing energy of the natural world like a sponge. *I hope he makes it*, I prayed to the sun as it sank over the horizon.

A couple of months later, we heard the news: Dave's tumor is operable! Called the Big Scoop, the fourteen-hour operation would take all the organs below his navel, leaving only his kidneys. Weeks of close observation in Houston were required after, so plans were made for Angels to accompany them on this voyage and they moved into a friends' apartment in Houston. Dave, ever mindful of Lois and her growing needs, asked them to be aware of her cognitive challenges while still honoring her autonomy. He explained to them, "Please, on a regular basis, ask her what she needs from you. If she doesn't respond with a clear need, you're welcome to prompt her by making a few suggestions, like, 'Do you need some food? A break? A walk? Can I take notes for you when the doctor's here? Can I do some cooking for you or for Dave?' Be sure to leave space for her to call up an answer. Remember, her rhythm is slower than yours. Please make sure to watch her closely—but without hovering!" *He's so good at balancing caregiving with respect for her need to control her own life. And, he's more concerned for her than for himself,* I thought. Again, I felt their symbiotic dance, their hearts entwined so sweetly. It occurred to me that their will to live was born from their desire to be there for each other...*THAT's what's keeping them alive.*

The White Flag of Surrender

Though Lois and Dave were never far from my mind and heart, with the second summer of camp looming, I was unable to go to Houston to support the Big Scoop. Then I got a call from Sally. In the doorway of my little pine cabin, I heard her shaky voice tell me, "Mom is in the hospital." I remembered back to mom's trip there a few months ago, when she had battled nurses and screamed as if she were being beaten until she was strapped down. *This isn't our accepting, large-mouth-laughing mother,* I'd thought as Sally held the cell phone aloft so I could hear the chaos.

I knew Sally could not face another round of that alone, so I immediately asked, "Do you need me to come?" With a great big sigh of gratitude, she answered, "Yes!" So, off to Baltimore I went, sleeping in the La-Z-Boy beside Mom, whose mitt-encased hands didn't stop her from trying to yank out IVs, but who was happy to see me and remembered I was her daughter. We stayed in the hospital until the blood clot had thinned, less than a week, but long enough for Mom to forget how to walk. Rejected for a return to residency at her Alzheimer's unit, we scrambled to find her a suitable home with skilled-nursing care. I thought about Lois and Dave and how they balanced the will to live with a willingness to surrender. I thought, *surrender is not giving up—it's giving* over. But I did not surrender easily. Sally and I were angry and frustrated, having just moved Mom into that unit. Under tremendous time pressure to get back to the demands of our lives, anger turned into bravado as we tag teamed twenty-four–seven Mom-care, passing the baton back and forth in a race to find her an acceptable bed (in a place *without* feces on the floor). We carried out our ancestral super power of doing, doing, and more doing. We drove all over tarnation, touring facilities on little sleep and lots of ice cream. Action covered our underlying fears. The ice cream soothed the savage beast of anticipatory loss. We were motherless children searching for a home for our mother. The act of searching blanketed a growing remorse that I'd be putting my mother in a nursing home. Phone calls with Lo, even as she faced Dave's imminent fourteen-hour surgery and her own limitations, added complexity to each day, but finally, The Triumvirate prevailed. Miraculously—and at the final hour—we found a place we loved. It was trustworthy, and they accepted us. Mom would not be shoved into a dirty corner but instead have a spacious room with a window looking out onto trees. That relief soon turned to cringes as I drove Mom to her new home and listened to her lament for the whole thirty minutes: "Please take me home…Please take me home…Please take me home…" Explaining that I couldn't because what had been home no longer existed wasn't something her shrinking brain could comprehend. So I drove with my heart in my mouth and surrendered to what I never imagined I would do. It was the right thing (*wasn't it?*). It would ensure quality care, kindness, and safety (*won't it?*). Still, with a great heaviness in my chest, my stomach in knots, and tears threatening, I said good-bye, then turned and walked away from my small, confused, and vulnerable mother sitting in a wheelchair. Even now, I believe it was the right thing to do—it was all I *could* do. Letting go of my mother that day was like waving a white flag. Like Lois and Dave, I'd surrendered to our suffering, accepting it as something to live with. *I have a choice*, I thought, *make friends with it or not, but it's not going away.*

My big-mouthed, laughing mother, Margie

With that choice stirring in the background, I returned to the camp fray, turning my full attention to a second season. Without my presence, Dave went under the knife while Lu, Ellen, and Angels flitted around Lo. He came through the surgery like a gold-medal winner, colostomy and urostomy bags reattached and the doctor saying it was all we could have hoped for. His recovery would take *more than a year*. Lois had held on through the long surgery, and, true to their souls' in-tandem nature, as soon as she saw him and was assured of his safety, promptly had a grand mal seizure. Assuming it was stress, the doctors increased her meds, and she put off further investigation until she and Dave could return to Austin together.

Meanwhile, my second round of camp turned into the summer from hell. Let's just say that a web of interpersonal dynamics erupted as financial concerns rose, and I laid off ten percent of staff and cut back salaries for the remaining wounded warriors. I carried out these instructions from the board of directors, though I heartily disagreed. I learned, firsthand, the meaning of the word "scapegoat." Negativity spread fast, like cancer cells, some people acting from fear, others from wounding, and still others from inadequate information. Far from perfect myself, I sacrificed time with my family and stood at the hub of the camp wheel, all spokes pointing toward me. Like my father, I'd abandoned those who needed me most, including myself.

As I identified more and more as the soldiering hero of CIC, Seth was losing patience with my long absences. But beyond that, my distraction and lack of presence, even when we were physically together, hurt him just as much. In his mind, sacrificing togetherness was only worth it if I felt fulfilled; my unhappiness just added fuel to his fire of feeling abandoned, and he patiently listened to my venting laments while his own needs went unmet. Little was left in my emotional bank account. Experiencing mistrust instead of support from the board, I became demanding and critical with the inadequacies of those around me. I was pissed off—beyond pissed off! Hardly at my best, I had no more ability to staunch the growth of the rage inside than I did to stop my sister's brain cancer. Pushed to my limit, I channeled my father, ranting at a board member over the phone, which stopped the conversation dead cold. We agreed to table the communication until camp was over for the season. In spite of the fact that we received rave reviews from both staff and campers, and were in solid fiscal shape after all, the summer ended on a seriously sour note. With pain carving into my heart as deeply as the canyon through which I drove, I navigated the winding road home.

Weary of mind, body, and emotion, I was home by Labor Day, where I would not be interrupted by emergencies or camp demands. I hunkered down behind a closed door to soothe my soul and get reacquainted with my lonely husband. I needed to sort through my anger and honestly assess my part of the conflict in which I'd lost the board's trust. To be more than a victim, I'd need to be accountable, which was easier said than done. While I contemplated how to do this, another much more imminent surrender awaited. We learned that Lois's seizure had not been caused by stress—she did, in fact, have another brain tumor, a mere year after the last.

Patience of a Saint

From that moment on, it was as if a tornado swept through our lives, touching down in one spot, then another, and another. Sally and Mom. Me and camp. Lois and Dave. Cancer and more cancer. *Will this never end?* Not to mention Seth, whose needs quietly simmered on the back burner. Having lost Cynthia, his twenty-year-long life partner, to cancer, then his father to mesothelioma, he understood the complexity of love and stress melded into one bundle better than most. He put on a compassionate and brave face as I struggled with disease at camp and in my family. Lois had her fourth brain tumor removed just after Labor Day, followed by weeks of inpatient rehab so she could relearn to walk. She needed to train her left hand for everything, as her right had atrophied. Dave's cancer regrew in a kidney, and he went to Houston for another surgery. With Angels and a shaky Lois by his side, true to their dance, Lois had another seizure in Dave's room as he emerged from anesthesia. Later, off balance in the parking lot, she fell and broke her left shoulder. *Holy crap!* Then it turned out Dave's cancer wasn't contained in the kidney—it had metastasized into his lungs.

I'd barely been home from my summer from hell when I realized I had to leave again—this time to go to Austin. Though it was a sacrifice, Seth supported my need to be there. I wanted it as much for me as for Lois. She needed help with everything, and Angels were needed more than ever. Getting on and off the toilet. Dressing, cooking, eating. And yet, she declined my offer to help. She had support. So-and-so would be there on Tuesday, then another friend on Wednesday, and blah-di-blah on Thursday, and by then Dave would be home. She seemed to forget that he'd just had surgery and would not be able to give her the help she needed. From her perspective, it was all covered; she didn't really need anything; she was going to be fine. I called Sally. "She can't even wipe her own ass," I said. "You're her Big Sister. Talk to her. Whatever it takes, get her to agree to my visit!" With a sardonic grin, I thought how Lois was like our fiercely independent father, who kept his power saw even in an assisted-living apartment. Mason was alive and well in Lois, too, not just me. Sally called back with the news that Lois had softened, then wept when it had dawned on her that that there was nothing like a sister for the intimacy of this moment. She said softly, "It would be good for Lil to come." I was grateful, sensing that the end was nearing.

Overarching Angel taxi service deposited me at Lo and Dave's just as Lo and her friend Francine (the Angel on duty) drove in from Houston. As we moved from cars to house, carrying suitcases and bags, Francine pulled me aside. She took a huge breath, leaned back against the limestone brick as if she could barely stand, and let go a huge sigh. She whispered, in the most solemn way, "I hope you have the patience of a saint." I chuckled, understanding immediately that she'd been referring to Lois's demanding style and perfectionist expectations. As it turned out, patience wasn't what I needed at all. Once it was just Lo and me, it turned into precious sister time, something we'd nearly forgotten. We fell into a rhythm together, thinking as one, like when we were little. I did her laundry and folded T-shirts to her specifications. I cooked our meals under her scrutiny and fed her tiny bites, which she chewed ad infinitum. We did errands, went to doctors, and got x-rays of her shoulder. I learned how to help her in and out of the car and to dress her without pain. I helped her on and off the toilet. I didn't give a snit about her directorial manner, and, yes, I wiped her bottom, exclaiming, "Lo, I'm wiping your butt!" and we laughed together at the absurdity of it. In spite of the trauma, tragedy, and troubles, we walked through the days lightly. Tears at the oncologist meeting aside, it was a rich time—a privacy of us. She was my little bird, and I feathered her nest.

During these days, we had some heart-to-heart talks. She had felt abandoned during the difficult summer, so I shared my summer-from-hell story. She listened to every detail. There was no criticism, no platitudes, no justifications—only empathy. She offered insight, saying, "Maybe in your passion to accomplish your tasks, you focused on the *doing* and forgot the *being*." As if past hurts no longer existed, I trusted her with my pain. We talked about our inherited impatience and lack of compassion for fallibility—both in ourselves and in others. We admitted to each other how perfectionism could tangle both of us in a spirit-killing approach to life. Seeing our father alive and well in each of us was, somehow, comforting. The more she held me without judgment, the more vulnerably I shared. We wove a sanctuary of trust then. It was beyond patience, beyond forgiveness, and I felt, for those few days, as if I was in pure (finally completely conflict-free) love with my sister. It was as if, in her surrender, she'd been stripped of whatever was not aligned with love. When I handed her a napkin and she started directing and giving instructions about what to do next, I said, "Who's *Little Daddy* now?" She laughed. I laughed. And I thought, *We've healed.*

Love, Healing, and Purpose

I was changed by that visit in a bigger way than the healing between Lo and me. Yes, cancer was a hurricane of needs in their house, but there was much more. So much love! When Dave came home, he was grateful I was there to support Lo, admitting that it gave him a feeling of freedom to know that, beyond Angels, she had a sister beside her. Over corn chips and salsa, he confessed, "Left to my own devices in Houston, I decided to visit the multiplex for an action movie." The image of him shuffle running across four lanes of traffic, colostomy bag sloshing while he held his recently stapled gut shut, got me laughing out loud. *Man, this guy's got some frickin' fortitude!* He went on, "It wasn't until I was committed—stuck on the median with cars zipping past on either side—that I considered my decision might have been the result of faulty thinking!"

"Was the movie worth it?" I asked. A mischievous grin told me all I needed to know. We stood in the kitchen while Lo napped, and he crunched his corn chips into corn meal, drifting into conversation about camp, purpose, and love. I told him about my recently discovered justice gene, the one Lois and I shared, which made us both rush into life holding a torch for the good and the right. Just like Dad. I admitted my shame, saying, "Even though my integrity, strength, and determination are qualities that help me succeed, they also keep me stuck. I set unreachable standards then judge myself and everyone else with perfectionist vitriol. No wonder people have been reactive to me." Acting the role of the hero was the family trance all over again. "Seeing all this is just painful," I told Dave. He listened as he munched. He then acknowledged my accountability and helped me see that I would also need to ask others to do the same. Take accountability but forgo the shame, he counseled. I could let go of perfectionism but still stand firm in my need for shared responsibility from others. I had not been alone in creating conflict, and my desire for mutual intro-spection was valid. I decided to bring a cautious respect toward the camp board and find out whether they, too, would try new behaviors. I let Dave in, as I had Lo. We listened to the ever-present doves outside the kitchen window while silently reflecting. Then I told him, "I think the purpose of your cancers has been to initi-ate Love into *all* of our lives." I shared the Hebrew phrase *Tikkun olam*, which means "repairing the world," pointing to humanity's shared responsibility of selfless service. *Their cancers are repairing the world—at least, right now they're helping me repair mine.* Dave had chosen social work as his career, to help troubled teens, and Lois had been an environmental educator, teaching the interrela-tionship between nature and humanity. But as we leaned against the counter filled with medications in a kitchen needing sweeping, I said, "Dave, I think yours and Lo's service to life is much bigger than your careers. I think that your cancer is linked to your life purpose. What's touched me so deeply with Lo over these past days isn't visible, it isn't outside us—it's love, which, as Lo says, is all that matters. And you are both living examples of love. That's your pur-pose. It's what you came here to learn, and it's what you came here to teach." We hugged wordlessly. As if ruminating on my words, his eyes turned inward, and he nodded to himself. I think he felt seen. Really, deeply seen.

That's when the distinction between healing and curing came into focus for me. Healing is what happens to the soul and spirit. Curing is fixing the broken physicality of that soul or spirit. For Lo and Dave, healing meant keeping true to their intention to reap joy from each moment, to do what made them feel alive, and to focus on their vitality of life while still forging forward with curative measures directed at their physical beings. For me, it meant becoming a more patient, kind, and conscious leader—transforming my approach as I had with Lo—and accepting the fallibility in all things and all people. The strength that Lois and Dave had been practicing and modeling wasn't from their will. It came from faith in something larger than themselves. They were special to so many people because they surrendered to the beauty of the heart, and love was a tangible force in their presence. I'd gone to support Lo and Dave and left supported by them instead.

The Dark of the Night

A couple of months later, tests revealed that, only three months after the fourth brain tumor, Lois had grown a fifth. Shortly before Thanksgiving, I was headed back to Austin for Lois's fifth brain surgery. As I packed my suitcase, my mind spun in a repeating loop: *It's only been three months...Holy fuck...Oh, man, her time is coming ...Three months! Shit!* Sally and I agreed that we needed to talk this over with Dave. We both felt it down to our bones—the specter of death hovered. I wanted to serve them, love them, and honor them, but I knew that as long as Dave was focused on miracles, Lois would do everything in her power to comply. We had to broach a conversation with Dave about surrender. Settling my gut, I prepared to say words no husband would ever want to hear.

The night before surgery, friends joined us for a chant. The harmonium began quietly, then gathered volume as its breathy voice built, sacred sound turning the room into our temple. I felt enlivened by our voices weaving, as if a powerful vortex of energy rose above us, and then I noticed a vibration at the center of my forehead, as if a stray hair were tickling my brow again and again. When I reached up to sweep it away, there was nothing there, just an ever-increasing vibration. When the chant ended, the pulsation slowly receded, and without many words, we each padded off to bed, where it occurred to me, *My third eye is cracking open*!

Early the next morning, Dave and I took Lo to the hospital, where we waited in an antiseptic anteroom for nurses to wheel a lighthearted Lo into surgery. While we waited, Lo asked me how I liked the chant. I told her about the crackling vibration, and she glowed in excitement as she said, "Wow. Shakti." The nurse came, we kissed good-bye, then reviewed the hand squeezes Dad had made up at her first surgery. Three times meant, "I love you." The reply, two squeezes, meant, "How much?" The final response, one long squeeeeeeze meant, "Mmmmmmmmm…this much!" That way, when she came out of her fifth brain surgery and words would be especially hard to find, we'd communicate by touch.

As I sat with Dave I realized, *He needs her—losing her is unimaginable to him.* I wanted to be careful with Dave's heart; I knew that talking about letting go would tear at its innermost chambers. But I also knew it had to happen and that I was the one who had to do it. Shakin' in my boots but keeping an even keel, I waited for the right moment, knowing Sally had my back and was on call at a moment's notice. Dave and I held vigil at the hospital as Lois slipped under anesthesia and we slid into a synergy of stillness, trying to meet her in the ozone layer or wherever she was flying. We meditated in vinyl hospital chairs, trying to keep restlessness at bay, then took turns leaving for short walks. We visited a nearby creek to soak up a breath of nature and went to the Seton League House—a quiet, caring inn for patients' families—where our room was fortified with healthy foods for the duration. Dave was holding on by a thread—sitting was becoming unbearably painful—but that did not stop him from being fully present for Lo. I reminded him to tend to himself, as he'd reminded the Angels who'd cared for Lo in Houston. I know he was grateful, even though he seemed to have no choice but to sit and wait for the surgeon to appear.

Several hours later, Dr. Kemper delivered his news cleanly and directly, as one would expect from a surgeon. His words sliced: "Surgery has gone as well as could be expected, but the cancer has spread, like fingers, across her brain. It's not possible to cut it all away." I thought I was prepared—it was what I'd expected—but the news landed with a thud on my chest. Intuition is one thing; facts are another. "Further surgery isn't possible without extensive damage. Her cancer is spreading." Crushed, Dave collapsed in on himself. We took one another's hands, then wrapped ourselves into each other and held on tight. I was quiet. Dave was angry. He said, "Why would he do that? Take all hope away?" I had no answer. His heart was aching and mine was racing. *How am I going to do this? I can't, I can't, I can't...*We spoke in whispers about what to do next, what to say to those praying for a successful outcome. I called Sally, who reminded me that I had the inner strength to say what I had to say; she would hold me up from afar. While Dave called Ellen, then Lu, I called Seth. Then the nurse motioned us into the ICU to see a groggy Lois. Watching Dave brighten when he lay eyes on her reminded me, *He's done this so many times before. Right now, everything is about helping her come back to this world.* I hid how terrified I felt to see her so emotionally flat. *Dave knows what she needs,* I thought as I followed his lead, cheering her on as she slowly fought her way out of the fog.

Only later, in the dark of the night, after Dave and I crawled into our respective twin beds, did the door of truth swing open. Ever so gently and ever so quietly, I said, "She's dying, Dave. The reason Dr. Kemper took away hope is because he's preparing us for what's next. She's not going to recover." I held my breath as I pulled the covers to my chin, certain that I'd upset him, afraid that I'd angered him. He was silent for a long time. I waited. Then quietly, he said, "Thank you for saying that. In my family, we're such cheerleaders. It's almost impossible to talk about these hard things." Having spoken the unspeakable, he could weep—we both did. The rest of the conversation is a blur, but I remember well the tenderness that passed between us as we realized that, together, we'd face the inevitable. Before we drifted off to sleep in our tiny twin beds, he said, "I'm grateful for your honesty, for the chance to explore this with you." The room was palpably filled with love, all tied up with sorrow, intimacy, and the deepest experience of brotherhood I'd known with Dave. When we agreed to walk side by side with Lo, Dave said, "We'll take it moment by moment by moment."

"I'm here for you all the way," was my soft reply.

The Dark of the Night Redux

Lo moved from ICU to a private room, Dave moved back home to Buda, and I camped at the League House, walking to the local coffee shop for an oversize muffin and latte each morning on my way to her room. Dave entrusted Lo to me, and I entrusted him to himself—at home where he could tend to his needs and return to work. Lo's hospital room gathered flowers, a small altar, and hospital food trays, which we often shared. She taught me how to order meals, and we laughed when she ate some Jell-O, which shocked me since both she and Dave were health-food fanatics. Lois was back in the land of the living, and I felt free to take walks when she napped or to head off to sleep when she dozed after Dave's evening visit. My number was on the white board in her room; nurses would call if something came up.

The phone startled me awake at two in the morning, rousing me from a triple Tylenol PM slumber. Instantly awake, I sat up. The nurse put a tearful Lo on the other end, and without a thought, I asked, "You want me there?" Through the receiver came a shaky "yes." I threw on clothes and ran; I could not get to her fast enough. I rushed into her room with a hug ready. In the dark of the night, she was having her own come-to-Jesus moment. Scared, she said, through her tears, "I'm dying." She knew it. And though I knew it, too—had said it to Dave, to Sally, and to myself—I could not bring myself to say it to Lo. *I'm not ready!* Not there, in the linoleum-floored, cinder-block–walled, curtain-draped room with monitors beeping and the soft squeak of rubber-soled shoes passing by. And so I said, "Well, not tonight, you're not." None of us were fully able to embrace the reality of death. Not yet.

I am so glad—glad beyond words—that I was there with her in that moment. I held her hand, listened to her fears, calmed her simply with my presence. It was OK with me if she cried, and she knew it. That made it possible for her to move past the crying. I didn't try to fix her or make her feel unafraid. I wrapped her in my arms. We chanted *Om Namah Shivaya* along with my iPod, sharing one set of earplugs. I positioned the vinyl La-Z-Boy alongside her bed, snuggling in it, still listening to the chant until, like babies, we both drifted into sleep holding hands. I cherish that dark night I shared with Lo—not her suffering but the memory of helping relieve her of it and the great depth of sisterly intimacy we shared. Looking back now, I often wonder what might have been different, in the events that followed, if I'd been able to affirm what Lo knew in her heart. When she said, "I'm dying," I just couldn't go there with her. Sometimes I wish that I had been more courageous that night...because I have the sinking sensation that it might have relieved an even greater suffering to honor the truth we all knew. Regretfully, Dave wasn't able to hold on to the realization that she was dying either; he continued to hope for a miracle with all his heart. Thus, much cheerleading ensued over the coming months.

The next morning, she was stronger of spirit but headed for rehab; she would have to start all over again, learning to walk with a walker and then a cane. Leaving her was wrenching, and as I prepared to go, Lo confessed, "I don't know if I have it in me to go through this again." In my heart, I wondered the same. I knew that she needed to hear birds outside her window and breathe fresh air again—that getting home was the most important thing. I told her I thought she was courageous. Her sharp response was, "What choice do I have?" *True,* I thought, but then said, "You could be bitter, resentful, or angry. But you aren't. That's courage. That's heart." Softening then, she said, "I'm not sure how much time I have left." Lois was completely tuned in to the reality of her body. As gently as I could, I replied, "Well…you'd better drink it all in then, Lo." She grew quiet, just looking at me for a long time. When I asked her what she was thinking, she said, "I'm drinking you in."

The Overarching Angel taxi service arrived to escort me to the airport. I didn't want to leave—I wanted to be with her forever and ever. After many tearful hugs, I looked her in the eye and, drawing on our shared scraped-knee childhoods, said, "I'm just gonna rip it off." We took one last long look at one another, and with fat tears creeping down her cheeks, she said, "Yup, rip it off." Without wanting to, and with sorrow carving a deeper chasm of love in my heart, I turned and walked out the door.

Section Three

Discovering Grace

Is there a greater human experience than to know love that is unbounded? To receive love in so many forms that I could actually feel it holding me? To be loved in such a way that it is never absent, only my awareness of it? To know love that transcends the challenges of physical disability, of chronic pain, and the insidious worries of cancer? To look into the eyes of another and have all these challenges dissolve under the power of the human heart?

For Lois and for me, as our physical challenges grow into a wide, fast-running river of needs, our pool of caring support has grown into an ocean of loving care, ever-present, always there in the ways and at the times we need, always asking to come in, to lighten the burden. As recipients of so much compassion from others, I'm learning compassion for these bodies our souls reside in, for all they've been through, how well they've served us. What a blessing our bodies are!

—Dave

Seven

Three Good-Byes

Lo's heart is so open; there is such beauty in her vulnerability.
Last week, she said, "It's just…that I thought…that I'd
have more time."

I know that our bodies will one day be left behind. By accepting this,
we are learning to find joy in any situation, even a hospital room,
and not to wait 'til this latest challenge passes.

I am learning to appreciate every moment we have and to cherish our
life together even more. Every day I'm thankful for the love
that we share.

—Dave

The Fire Blazes

About a month after Lo's surgery, I was home, and life had begun returning to normal. My meeting with the camp board had produced positive results; everyone was working hard to grow, and I'd received the support I needed. Then Dave gave us the great news that Lo would soon be coming home from rehab. Hallelujah! Angels showed up to raise the couch and bed to the proper height. She learned how to shower safely and to maneuver a walker. Ramps were built and floors cleared for wheelchair access as needed. Angels stayed with Lois while Dave was at work, and Lo surrendered to what had become inevitable—someone had to be with her twenty-four hours a day for safety. Dave brought his beloved home just in time for New Year's Eve, which they spent in front of a blazing fireplace. Sal had come to Oakland for the holiday, and together, we felt warmth and joy through voice mail when we heard their made-up New Year's song to the tune of "Happy Birthday." "Felize ano nuevo, aqui… Felize ano nuevo, a-a-aqui-i-i…Felize ano nue-e-e-vo, a-a-a-qui-i-i… Felize ano nuevo, aqui!" Their harmonies lifted our spirits, and we replayed it about a thousand times. Though we no longer believed in the possibility of a full recovery, our hope for Lo and Dave was that they return to some kind of normalcy in the New Year. Our fingers were crossed as Sally, Seth, and I laid 2009 to rest.

It wasn't to be. Dave's next visit to MD Anderson revealed a shift in his diagnosis: terminal. There was nothing more medical science could do. Bravely, Dave faced the reality that he had, at most, a year and a half to live and went home to deliver the news to Lois. He told the rest of us, "This is where I remind myself of the importance of living each day to the fullest. The moment is all we've got anyhow."

Of course, in their uncanny in-tandem cancer journey, life had something else in store. Lois had fallen over backward onto the kitchen floor while Dave was at his appointment. He returned to find her resting but in considerable pain. A middle-of-the-night call to the doctor and a trip to the ER revealed that Lo had broken her back. Though he had shared his news with her, processing their new reality would need to take a backseat to Lo's more urgent situation. She was fitted for a full-torso brace, cinched so tight she could barely catch a deep breath; it held her upright and kept her back safe. We called it her turtle shell. With more injuries at stake, sadly, Lo went back into rehab. She was unable to walk or maneuver without help from aides.

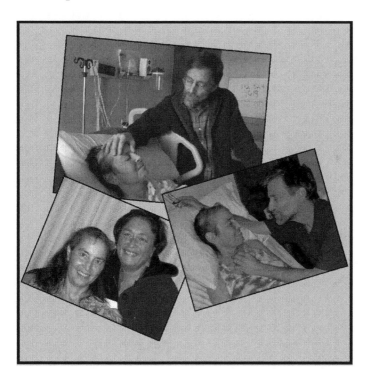

Hospital Lovin':
Dave with Lo at the hospital and rehab
Sally with Lo at Rehab

Sally and I took turns visiting, overlapping when we could. We boosted Lo's morale and allowed Dave to vent and sort out what to do next. When Sally coined the phrase, "Helping Lojo find her mojo," the two of us fell right into our roles, a great tag team, reminding Dave to rest, bringing Lo's favorite foods, tidying flowers, and folding laundry. We bustled around her, avid cheerleaders, or filled the room with meditative silence, then wheeled her to physical therapy. When she struggled to walk the entire hallway, I suggested that she imagine Dave, and home, at the end of the corridor. That got her motivated! We ran gentle interference when she and Dave bickered. We took latte breaks when Lo napped. When their friend Elaine cooked up a tray of steamy enchiladas with freshly made corn tortillas, homemade black beans, and brown rice, we feasted and recalled memories of the Magothy, regaling Lo with stories to lift her spirits. Sally and I held each other up, too, weaving our best blanket of presence and peace.

Dave decided to leave his job (insurance be damned!) so that he could devote himself to self-care along with spending time with Lo. He wanted to have energy to reap the rewards of spiritual study, which had been hard to fit into a schedule filled with work to rehab to sleep to work. He'd spend the rest of his days enjoying his home sanctuary, surrounded by birdsong and wandering deer. The leave-taking from work boosted his spirits. During his last weeks, students came to tell him what an important force he'd been in their lives. He recounted the story of the middle school boy who'd shown up religiously for his sessions but never spoke a word. Dave did all the talking for months as he puzzled at how to get this troubled boy to open up. Without dialog, Dave feared nothing would happen.

One day he suggested they go for a walk, grabbing a Frisbee in a last-minute brainstorm as he stepped out the door. Dave still talked, lightly tossing and catching the Frisbee as they walked, then, sneakily, he let it fall to the ground. Eventually the young man reached for the Frisbee and Dave inched farther away until they were in a full-blown game—tossing it back and forth for the entire counseling session. Soon after, the young man started talking and never stopped; the healing had begun. Dave loved his job and told story after story like the one above. He made a huge difference in the lives of the students he'd served, and as he prepared to leave, teachers, fellow counselors, and students put together a small scrapbook of letters thanking him for his steady, kind, inspirational, and fun-loving collegiality. One young man showed up out of the blue and revealed that he attributed graduating from high school and getting into college completely to Dave, who savored the gratitude as he said good-bye to that part of his life and identity. It was sad but poignant and ultimately a relief to let go of outer concerns, turning toward what really mattered most—love.

Lambchops

Each evening at the rehab center, I waited until Lois drifted off to sleep before returning to their house, where Dave and I would often sit up late and discuss details of the day. As we spent more and more time together we would occasionally bump heads. One particular evening, we were alone in the dusk, sitting quietly in our rocking chairs in front of the fireplace when he turned and said, "I have something I want to talk about with you." I was immediately nervous, steeling myself as he told me that for years he'd thought of me as a bull in a china shop. He recounted specific moments in our history: when I harvested broccoli from the garden without asking permission; when I changed the music at their wedding; when I jumped ahead of the hospice social worker to ask Lo what she wanted to complete before dying. He recounted each item slowly, as I worked hard to stay centered. I knew his words were true, but not the whole truth. And it was hard to take in feedback as I gave myself generously in service to their lives. I took deep breaths as I tried putting my feelings aside, reminding myself that he had lost his partner and was, himself, dying. Though Lo was still alive, she simply could not be there to help him face his impending death. He was lonely for her. He was deeply tired. And this conversation moved at an agonizing pace.

We each rocked back and forth, the creak of the wooden rockers filling the spaces as I listened without defending. Then Dave surprised me with, "I see now that I was wrong about that. I've come to understand your heart. You aren't a bull in a china shop. You're more like a lamb in a china shop." I smiled, and he took my hand, saying, "I'm such a perfectionist. I have so little control over my life that sometimes I overdo it, trying to find control where I can. Little things end up meaning a lot to me." He told me about taking things too literally so that his expectations were often dashed and about getting caught up in doing rather than being. He talked about his drive to make sure everything met his standards, feeling that he could never really rest. He acknowledged that he often had an agenda that could never be met, then blamed others for not meeting it. I sat there and marveled at the dovetail of our personality traits. Dave and I had not talked like this before. He said, "I couldn't see you as you are, Lil, and for that I'm sorry. I love you. You truly are as soft as a lamb."

My heart burst. I thanked him and said, with a sly grin, "Well, I am a bull in a china shop, sometimes." He chuckled, and I followed with, "But I have the best of intentions, however poorly they may come across. I'm learning that sometimes I do railroad over people." We sat together in mutual love and respect. "I'm a whole lot like you, Dave. I'm a perfectionist, too. But being seen as more than that feels really good."

He said, "I love the sisterhood that you and Sal bring to me. This would all be much more daunting without you two—your help and the love you bring into our lives. You have always made your commitment to us clear, and it gives us comfort and strength to know that. I sense that the power of three is especially important right now. We have called upon you and we will again. You've taught us so much by giving without expectation of return. I want to say thank you, which doesn't quite capture it, but thank you!"

Wow. Wow! I felt so seen by him that night. So known and recognized in my true nature. That was the moment I started thinking of him as my brother, not just my brother-in-law; we'd become brother and sister of the heart. Later I found a note he'd scribbled to himself on a torn scrap of paper.

Legacy:
Love of family, friends, and community
Others experience God, as God speaks through this life
A clean wake behind
Material support to loved ones

I now realize that in speaking his heart to me that night, Dave was leaving a clean wake behind. He was clearing up relationships through the lens of his heart. Would we have had these healing moments if cancer had not entered our lives? Death's approach showed us what mattered. We cherished each other. From then on, I signed my e-mails, "Love, Lambchops."

The Sun at My Feet

As fire blazed through Dave and Lois's lives, Sal and I continued our conversation about how to get Lo home where she could be more at peace in her spirit. We thought it was time for hospice. Dave was reticent to release life-saving treatments, even though Sally and I felt it was time to look toward ease and comfort. I'd brought this up to him and he was clear; it wasn't time. Sally and I waited. Intuitively, we knew it was our role to help them accept the inevitable. But how? When? What was the right timing? We were asking just these questions one day during a hurried phone conversation on my way to work. From the corner of my awareness, I recognized a tarot card upside down in the street, pockmarked from recent rains. I scurried on in the crisp air and then stopped cold when it registered that wisdom was being offered from the universe. I interrupted Sally midsentence to exclaim, "Whoa! There's a tarot card in the gutter!" Sally's immediate response was, "Well, pick it up!"

So I scooped up the weather-beaten card and turned it over to find The Sun card of the Aleister Crowley deck. I described it to

Sally as she looked it up on Google. "There's a blossoming rose at the center of the sun, with twelve rays reaching outward, connecting to the twelve zodiac symbols. A rainbow halo surrounds the sun's glow, and there are two cherubs suspended in front of a mountain with a ring around it—possibly a snake." As I stood on the curb in front of my office, we began interpreting the card as an answer to our questions. We felt like we'd been given a gift once we understood that The Sun card is about celebrating the cycles of life. It stands for the reconstruction that comes in response to destruction, just as rebirth comes from death. We felt a great sense of the sacred in the card, as if the cyclical journey of transformation within the larger-than-human worlds was talking to us. We read the card as a message showing us the wholeness of existence—that life, death, and rebirth are all part of the same natural cycle. The story of finding The Sun card would be our way into conversation with Lo and Dave. When we shared it with them, we all agreed, the theme was of transcendence and of a new life coming from the destruction of the old. As we looked further into the card, Sally and I began to understand that The Sun was guiding us to see death of the physical body as a birth of the spirit body. In addition to helping Lois's physical body let go and die, we'd be helping her spirit be reborn. Sally noticed a Hebrew letter, Resh, at the bottom of the card. She told me, "Hebrew is a sacred alphabet that was used to represent the divine. In the ancient, mystical teachings of the Kabbalah, the letter Resh represents the head—the place of divine illumination." She went on, "The number of the card is nineteen, which, in numerology, reduces to a one, meaning God, the One." *Wow!* I thought. *It's all coming together, telling us the same thing in so many different ways!* I told Sally that the card reminded me of the image of the still blue lake at the end of Lo's big dream. Lois had interpreted the lake as the blue pearl, a state of spiritual transcendence or what some might call heaven. More than just abstract ideas, The Sun card and the dream were telling us to prepare for Lo's final transformation, prepping us to be midwives for an encounter with death and spiritual rebirth. We needed to get ready for Lois to die.

Free to Soar

Integrating that understanding with daily life was no easy task. I worked on healing the rift with the Camps in Common board while Sally carried on with Mom, who was by then completely submerged into Alzheimer's. Sadly, she was unable even to string words into a coherent sentence. Phone calls consisted of my shouting, "Mom!" loudly and repeatedly until I could break through her ranting. Finally she'd emerge from her fog and recognize me as one of her people. Then her voice would soften, often with a lilting "oooh!" She would deliver strings of words, only loosely described as conversation, her tone rising and falling with stories. Sometimes she told me funny ones, and I'd laugh with her. Other times she was mad, telling me all about it. Though I had no idea what she was saying in any ordinary sense, I followed her tone and acted as if I did, responding with, "Oh my!" or, "Really?" or, "Yeah, I understand, Ma." The aides told Sally how much calmer she was after a call from one of her daughters or after Sally's twice-a-week visits. I planned to visit soon, suspecting it would be my last chance to see her alive.

But I needed to see Lo first. I put off my visit to Mom and went to Texas instead, then had returned home just in time to celebrate Seth's birthday, when the phone startled me awake at six in the morning. *This can't be good*, I thought, looking at the caller ID and telling Seth, "It's Sally." I answered the phone with trepidation, remembering the hospital visits of the past year. "Hey. What's going on?" A long pause. "Mom died." Silence. With a sharp intake of breath, I realized that the opportunity for a good-bye visit was gone. Seth, lying quietly beside me, surrendered his needs once more as he listened to the news on speaker phone. "They think it was a heart attack. I'm heading over there now to sit with her body," Sally said.

We talked briefly, and one of us said, "Well, she's free now." We agreed that it wasn't much of a life anymore and that, in spite of feeling deeply saddened, we were relieved, too. We agreed on the importance of a brief ceremony to help release Mom's spirit, which we would do once Sally was in Mom's room. But first we had to decide how and when to tell our fragile, vulnerable Lo. Picturing her in her bed at rehab, alone and unable to move, we wondered if we should call Dave first so that he could be at her side when we gave her the news. We also put ourselves in her shoes... shoes that commanded respect, dignity, and no pity. Were they upon our own feet, these shoes would demand to walk as an equal partner in the journey. We agreed. Lois needed to be part of the shared story, no matter how difficult. I called Dave while Sal called Lo. Seth was spacious; what choice did he have? I'd just lost my mother. But inside, he was hurting, another important moment gone uncelebrated.

Then we three sisters, in Triumvirate style, held a conference call once Sally was at Mom's bedside. In virtual space, Sally laughed as she held the cell phone out to the room and we created our good-bye. We proclaimed our love, expressed gratitude for good mothering, and shared our sorrow for Mom's sudden departure. We encouraged our mother's spirit to soar. We shared tears and silence. We were not sad that Mom was released from the body and mind which no longer gave her pleasure or quality of life. Still, facing a reality where we could no longer see her, sit next to her, or hug her lay heavy in our chests. Softly, from three different cities, our triangle of love touched the empty places in our hearts and surrounded Margie's body until there was no more to say.

Lo couldn't be in Baltimore for the memorial, but she was still part of planning the ceremony and e-mailed a video of her eulogy. Like at Dad's memorial, I cried harder while watching Lo struggle to speak, bound tightly in her turtle shell, haltingly reading the cardboard cue cards Dave held. She shared how, as a teen, she'd lied to Mom about going to the drive-in with a boy, then confessed in tears, only to be told, "I never said you couldn't go to the drive-in!" Throughout the video, Lo slurped at an ice-cream cone, each time slurring, "Have I mentioned that Mom loved ice cream?" It was sweet and funny and sad all rolled up in one bundle. Sally and I held hands and blew our noses, a pile of wet tissues growing in our laps as Seth handled logistics of the day. Our hands tightened as we watched, knowing that we were grieving Lois's losses and Mom's passage, both. We celebrated with homemade ice-cream sandwiches at the end of the ceremony, because as Lo had said, to know Margie was to know she LOVED ice cream. Since Lo and

Dave were there with the miracle of Skype, each cousin visited her, one by one, in a cozy corner we'd set up. Lois didn't speak many words, but she was shining and fully present, so happy to see each member of our family. In spite of her turtle-shell body cast, the crazy-wacky-uneven hair-loss hairdo barely covered with a colorful straw hat sitting askew, and extreme fatigue, the gentle golden aura of Lois Joy was miraculously, tangibly, peacefully exuded through the computer screen. Everyone commented on her exceptional beauty, and I thought, *She truly has become love embodied.*

Lo's crazy wacky haircut by Ellen
Lo in turtle shell with Dave on Skype call at Mom's memorial

Lojo Loses her Mojo

The beauty of the ceremony lifted us, but soon the loss sucked the remaining wind right out of Lois's sails. She called one day while I was at work. Chair swiveled to the corner for privacy, feet tucked up against the wall beneath the Defenders of Wildlife calendar, I heard Lo say, "The brain cancer has metastasized into my spine. The doctor says it is really rare with this particular strain."

I was speechless. I knew she needed my words, but what to say? I scrambled, searching, and then words came, "Well, you *are* a rare bird, Lo." Though typically it took her a long time to formulate words, without missing a single beat, she said, "That's the name of our book! *Two Rare Birds!*"

"Oh, Lo, how *perfect!*" I replied, thinking...*that's not likely to get written now...*

A few days later, Dave called to tell me, "The docs say that Lo has a few weeks to live." He was stunned. In spite of our conversation in the dark of the night, he'd convinced himself that she would bounce back like the Lo of the past. With that magical thinking, he'd been planning that he would go first, and had been busy making financial arrangements for Lo to go on without him. As he wrapped his mind around the reality that she would die before him, deep loneliness set in, and sorrow laid a shroud over us as we talked logistics. When we hung up, the world took on a different sheen; nothing seemed quite the same as it had a moment ago. There was a kind of transparent wave in front of everything, as if the fragility of the world were revealed. I was suddenly aware of the limitations of time, how life goes by in a flash. I looked at people on the street, thinking, *That person will die one day, too.* Seeing kids playing on tricycles, watching their joy, I thought, *They will die one day, too.* Then the thought came, *I will die one day, too.* What had been a concept on the day The Sun card appeared at my feet came completely into focus: that earthly life is a cycle, and it would include an ending, a real, finite ending. What had been an intuition became fact. *Lois's life is cycling to its end. Death is real.* Later, cocooned again at my desk, I called Lo, needing to hear her voice. "I guess I wanted to beat Dave," she said.

"I guess you did," were the only words I could think of in reply.

Dave, thankfully, found Adele, the perfect, able-bodied caregiver, so that, with her presence and help from hospice, Lo was able to go home. Strong and capable, Adele flowed easily into the rhythm of their lives. When Dave told the news to their larger community, he said, "We know that our spirits live on after all this, but I am terribly sad at the thought of losing sweet Lois and losing our lives as we've known them. Our love will live on beyond these bodies, yet the thought of not having Lo in my daily life brings me to tears." I knew I had to be there beside them— there was nowhere else I could be—for what was to come in the next weeks. And Sally did, too.

The three of us took turns spending the night with Lo. I learned to move quickly but smoothly in order to get the bedpan in place when she whispered me awake with, "Lil! Lil! I have to pee." It became a sleeping meditation—getting up, tending to her, falling back to sleep, then doing it again a couple hours later. Occasionally we'd talk for a bit before falling back to sleep, sometimes holding hands, always whispering in the darkness of the night. Once, Dave and I were both holding midnight vigil for Lo when she could not sleep. As we sat quietly, Dave asked her in a sweet, soft voice, "What do you want your memorial to be like?"

She pondered, then slowly answered, "I don't know."

I suggested, "Lo, your memorial will be about celebrating your legacy."

Her reply, "What *is* my legacy?" She really had no idea. In the quiet, dark night, Dave and I began telling Lo what we thought she was leaving to the world: beautiful pottery, inspiring people to care for the earth, ushering youth into nature, touching the world with her creativity and collage, feeding birds, and protecting native plants. She took it all in but settled only after I told her, "You reminded us over and over about the most important thing: Love. You helped so many of us open to love." Touched, she nodded. Then she said, forcefully, "I want my girlfriends—Ellen, Ann, Lauren, April, and Terri—to plan my memorial."

Dave and I promised we would see to it. Soothed by the intimacy of that moment, we each drifted off to our separate dream worlds, knowing that we'd shared an important moment helping Lo begin to separate from this life.

Taking Matters into Her Own Hands

The house became a temple of quiet. We spoke in whispers all day long, preparing to midwife Lois into whatever was next for her spirit. Friends and family came and went, some from out of state, saying good-bye. When we realized there were many more people who wanted to say good-bye than Lo had energy for, we decided to hold a chant and let Lois decide whether she felt up to individual visits. Twenty or thirty people came, bearing pot-luck dishes and chai tea, filling the space with their love, tears, and laughter. There was lots of hugging and milling about, then we settled into what was more of a clump than a circle, spill-ing into the hallway and dining area. Lois, in her hospital bed, closed her eyes and turned inward during the chant. Baritone voices blended with alto and soprano, sweeping over us as one melodious whole. Lois seemed to walk right up to the edge of the underworld, as if peering into the Great Beyond. After the sing-ing, Dave brought friends, one by one, into her room, and Lois opened her eyes in greeting, wordlessly allowing each person to express his or her unique form of a good-bye. Later, with just the two of us in the room, she turned to me and said, "I don't know how to die."

I mused, "I think it has to do with surrender."

As fat tears pooled on the pillow, Lois said, "You always make me cry, Lil," and then asked for Dr. Philip, their close friend, spiri-tual compatriot, and auyervedic doctor. It was a closed-door meet-ing, after which she invited us in to announce that she'd "decided to die." She was ready to stop eating and drinking. She planned a final meal, but after that, she would only take food or drink neces-sary for absorbing the needed medications. Dr. Philip sat between Sally and me on the couch and prepared us for what was to come. He said that because Lo was willfully urging her death forward rather than waiting for it to happen naturally, the dying process would be intensified and would probably take around five days to complete. He told us that her body would begin a yogic breath, much like kundalini breathing, raising enough energy for her soul to leave her body through the top of her head—her crown. We were ready. We prepared ourselves for the vigil.

Amazingly, she lingered for ten days. If it is true that people die as they lived, Lois is an example of that principle. Her strong will kept her alive with brain cancer for fourteen years, and letting go was easier said than done. Surrendering her commitment to life felt like trying to pry open a fist that had been held tight for a decade and a half; the slow release of clenched fingers was excruciating. Sometimes she was so deeply anxious, she'd lash out, sending Sally from the room with, "You make a racket!" or grabbing my earring, nearly yanking it out as she exclaimed, "I just can't stand this one more minute!" I'd spend afternoons by her bed in the rocking chair until she drifted into sleep. Quietly, I'd slip out, peeking in a couple minutes later to find her eyes wide open, imploring me to return to the chair or to cuddle her on the bed. Letting go was not just a matter of the physical body or the mind; it was a ceremony of the whole psyche. Sally, Dave, and I—Dave, an honorary member of the new Triumvirate—held each other's hands and hearts through this terrible tension. She was wrestling with the Angel of Death tenaciously, trying to surrender but holding on for dear life all at the same time. For someone in her condition to live for ten days without food or water was a testament to her strength of spirit. I kept thinking, *Dying is not for the faint of heart!*

As Lois headed into what hospice called the "active-dying phase," any assumptions I had about death being beautiful were blown to bits; I felt humbled to my core as tension and anxiety grew. I made sense of it by thinking about the nine months of gestation inside a womb. If that's how long it took for her spirit to fully attach to a fetus, to grow into a body and be pushed through a tiny canal during hours of labor, then of course it could be just as difficult to leave. And this physical world, where she'd been for nearly sixty years, with all its pleasures and pains—relationships, sunsets, loneliness, mountain tops, sensuality, heartache—is a lot to release. Why, of course she'd become quite attached to this body through which she'd experienced it all! Lois was doing her last bit of soul work on the earthly plane—detaching from that used-up body for whatever new life lay beyond—and she was going to grapple as long as she needed. Sitting beside Lois's deathbed, I learned that love is not, as some would say, an absence of fear but a choice to face the fear with grace. Slowly, Lois began to surrender. Her eyes grew larger, rounder, and more full. Words became mostly a thing of the past, but her communication of the heart was loud and clear as small slices of time turned into larger and larger chunks in which everything but love was suspended.

In one of these moments, I was running my fingers through her little bit of hair—what we called Lo's topknot. (A topknot is a birder's phrase for the feathered crown some birds have, like blue jays or woodpeckers.) As I combed her topknot, Lois turned her big brown eyes to me and said, with a hint of humor, "Now *you* get to make the spring curl." We smiled, remembering our beauty-parlor games from so long ago, and my eyes welled as we drank in the pleasure of one another. So much had healed between us.

Lois exerted her right to choose how she wanted to go, right up through these last days as she gave herself over to love entirely; she'd reached a kind of surrender that is hard to fathom. Even on her deathbed, she exuded a kind of indescribable light. She was almost nonverbal, nearly completely paralyzed, and in tremendous pain, yet still radiant and glowing. Though it will sound like overkill, she was beatific. Being with her was compelling. What had mattered most became tangible, as love filled her room. Divine, beautiful Love.

Labor

Sally and I were out on a break when she picked up her cell phone. She said, "OK, we'll be right there." She hung up and whispered, "It's time." We hugged tearfully, then sprang into action. Our silent, five-minute drive felt like twenty with the intention to midwife Lois into the next world filling every cell of our bodies. We stopped at the doorstep to gather our wits and enter the moment consciously, respecting the sacredness of Lois's passage. We looked at one another then stepped across the threshold, into the haven where Lois lay, breathing the breath of fire, just as Dr. Philip had described. Dave's relief at seeing us was palpable. He said, "Do you think this is it?"

"Yes." The three of us gathered in a silent embrace. We knew, intuitively, to surround her, as people have done for all time. Dave stood at her feet, Sally and I at either side. Lo's head was turned toward the window with eyes open but not seeing—at least not anything of this world. Her breathing intensified, with a quiet inhale and forceful exhale. Ever so gently, I touched her and whispered, "Lo, it's Lil. I'm here." Like in childbirth, her body knew just what to do. Dave told her she was doing a good job, then the three of us became silent. Our unspoken intention was to bear witness to this holy act as she gathered steam to birth herself into the Great Beyond, whatever that may be. We trusted Lois to know exactly how to die.

Shifting to more comfortable positions, Sally and I sat with Dave lying beside us while Lo labored. The only sounds were the CD of Gurumayi's soft chanting and Lois's breath. I watched. I listened. I was reminded of the Lamaze breath, which accompanies each contraction of birth labor. I sat in wonder of this mystery. I leaned over, bowing my head toward my heart, humbled by the sacred moment, the cusp of life and death, whose thin line would be drawn between Lois alive and then not. She stopped breathing. Internally, I counted the seconds, up to twenty, and then she started up again. Not yet. Not enough steam. Patience reversed time so that what felt like mere moments stacked on top of each other turned into an hour and a half. Several times her breathing stopped. Each time I counted. Each time, twenty was the limit. It seemed as if she was searching for the path out of her body, each pause between breaths a contraction through which Lois was birthing herself into another level of consciousness. Like in the final moments of childbirth, I thought to myself, "Push!" Lois's breath finally became quieter, more refined, then almost imperceptibly, it stopped altogether. We sat in stillness, the only sound our own breathing until, slowly, Dave moved to her side. He laid a kiss on her forehead then leaned into Sally and me as his grief spilled onto our shoulders in loud sobs. She was, indeed, truly gone.

Cleansing Rituals

We had been present to the mystery of life and death. We'd witnessed the birth of a soul moving out of life—from incarnation to dis-incarnation. Sally told me that she, too, had thought, "Push!" as Lo's spirit moved out of her body. She had a vision of two hands at Lo's crown, waiting to greet her spirit being born into another reality. Sally and I transitioned into ceremonial action in dreamlike harmony when Dave returned to the room with essential oils in a warm tub of water. He left us to wordlessly carry out an innately known ancient ritual. In sync, we slid into an honored ancestral pattern, as we had with our father's body, moving beyond conscious knowing to lovingly wash the empty chrysalis of Lois's spirit—her body. We dressed her in beauty, with a thick garland of red, orange, and yellow marigolds— brought from the Siddha Yogis just days prior— laid in a halo around her face.

Lois was gone. We felt huge relief; it was like letting go of a big sigh after holding our breath for weeks of tending. With tears and gratitude we acknowledged that she was free from that used up body, and every conversation, every action was tempered with exhaustion. We moved through the house, first waiting for the hospice nurse, then the Neptune Society (to come for Lo's body) in a surreal state of being, as if we, too, were standing at the gates of the Beyond. A veil *had* parted and we'd touched the ephemeral lands of spirit, and the sacredness of the passage we'd witnessed stayed with us. Dave, Sal, and I agreed that the trauma of dying is like the trauma of birth, but not just for the person making the transition.

For all three of us, who were Lois's guides on that journey, it was rocky and rigorous. But love had prevailed, sealing our hearts to each other. And we each needed to grieve, and heal, in our own, unique ways.

Though Sal and I were loathe to leave, we desperately needed to return to our lives; we'd been gone nearly a month. Summer was about to begin, and we had our respective camps to run. Even though I felt the loss of my sister in my skin and wanted to be there for Dave, I needed to go. But before leaving, we hosted a house cleansing to help Dave begin his life without Lo. Though terminal, Dave still had many months ahead of him, and we hoped that a freshened space would support his mourning process. The Angels showed up en masse to help cleanse the house from top to bottom. Furniture was rearranged, cobwebs dusted out of corners, and ceiling fans wiped clean. Everyone had a favorite Lois story to share. Terri, Lois's girlfriend and best bird buddy, filled the bird feeders (as she'd promised Lois she would) then told me a hilarious tale. She and Lo had headed out one day in hopes of spotting a golden-cheeked warbler, an endangered species. As birders often do, they waited for a very long time, and when they eventually needed to pee, they each went their separate ways into the bush. That was when Terri heard Lo's urgent whisper, "I've got one!" Terri scurried around the scrub oaks to join her and was astonished to find Lois standing upright, binocs glued to her eyes with purple pants pooled around her ankles. What joy I felt in that memory! Sally and I departed knowing that Lois's memorial was in wise and loving hands.

Celebration of Life

A month later, we returned for Lo's memorial celebration at Westcave Preserve. Built of stone and glass, the visitor center was a sanctuary in the hills of Travis County, Texas. It could only be reached via a long road that wound past open meadows, then through dripping strata of rock beside river crossings. Since Lois had worked with Westcave on a curriculum for Camp El Ranchito, bringing underserved youth into nature, the board of the preserve graciously offered the space for her memorial. With over two hundred guests, Lo's girlfriends helped Dave create a true celebration! Beyond the ceremony and slide show eulogizing her life, they laid out her lifetime collection of bird, art, nature-poetry, and environmental awareness books, inviting guests to take something home as a treasured token. Incredible homemade food graced the table, and Dave made a playlist of danceable music, asking us to push back chairs and dance to Chris Williamson's "Song of the Soul," Lo's favorite. I treasured the slide show (even though I cried through the entire thing), which included a video of toddler Lo, then a dance performance, and then Lo in a park-ranger uniform teaching a bunch of inner-city kids the antics of a barn owl. Much like the chicken dance that had once triggered a lifetime of jealousy, Lois completely *became* the owl. But this time, I was not jealous; I just loved her. Dave flitted about as if at a wedding, despite sobbing on Lu's, then Sally's and my shoulders a few hours earlier. He had fully entered his sorrow *and* his joy.

Over the next several months, Dave wrote many letters to Lo. This one is perhaps the most touching:

Dear, sweet Lois,

I want you to know that I enjoyed, so much, *the celebration of your precious life on June 5th. My heart felt your presence in every part of the celebration. I saw your smile in the shining faces of all who gathered together in their love for you. I continue to celebrate you every day, some days with a smile, some days with tears. Most days with both. Until we unite in the dance of the spirit, I remain with endless gratitude for the gift that is you.*

Dave

I returned to another summer season of camp but kept closely connected to Dave. I created a small shrine beside a rushing waterfall on icy-cold Spanish Creek. I built rock cairns in a wild and secluded spot along its rocky banks where Indian rhubarb grows. The large-leafed greens, often picked by campers and placed upside down on their heads for umbrella-like hats, created a lush space where I meditated or reached out to Dave via cell phone. I'd promised Lois that I would be there for him; it settled in me like a vow. Plus, being there for him was a lot like being there for myself. Every week on my day off, I'd call Dave, who invariably answered with, "Hey, Lil, it must be Wednesday!" Hunkering down in the grass, we'd talk about everything and nothing. He'd cry, I'd cry, and we'd hold each other in virtual arms for a brief time.

As Dave grieved, he also turned his attention to his own well-being, taking steps that made a tremendous difference in his healing. He found the best pain-management doctor in Austin (who, as it turned out, was also a hospice medical director). The doctor immediately rearranged Dave's medications until his pain level was better than it had been in over a year. This made for *big* quality-of-life changes—with reduced pain came more clarity of mind and restored energy. He deepened his spiritual practices, spent overnights each week with friends Ann and Dr. Philip in their Wimberley home, and flourished with visits from vibrant nieces and nephews. Dave's spirit grew stronger. He lived with complete abandon, giving himself to his true nature, where generosity was the guiding hand on his heart.

The Frio

It wasn't always that way. Dave and Lo were frugal, possibly to a fault. It had begun early for both of them. Lois saved more than money; in July she could dig out hidden Halloween candy from her jewelry box for a summer treat. As a teen, Dave put away every penny just as meticulously as he cared for his stamp and rare-coin collections. As their diseases progressed, their thrifty ways were not without reason; they knew a day might come when assisted living or mounting medical bills could topple their comfortable but decidedly *not* conspicuously consumptive existence. But once Lo died and Dave's days were numbered, the stockpile took on a completely different meaning. With grand gestures of generosity, he gave large sums to his twenty-three nieces and nephews and turned away Lois's inheritance from my mom; this financial gift meant the world to Sally and me. But to Lu, he said, "I've got this pile of money, and I can't take it, or any of these physical things, with me. I want to do something fun!" He talked about coming to the Bay Area for a visit to the Siddha Yoga Ashram and to take Lu to the Pacific where we'd spread Mason's ashes. He wanted to show her where he and Lo had walked with Sally, Seth, and me, where his spirit had been renewed among the ancient, giant redwoods of Armstrong Woods. But his strength was waning, and a trip of that magnitude was too much. Instead, Lu made a soft bed in the back of her SUV, complete with pillows, a virtual Arabian tent of luxury. With a box and cooler filled with Dave's favorite road foods, including the Dr. Pepper he'd started sipping after years of rejecting all sodas, she drove the five hours from Sherman to Austin and loaded him into her loving embrace for a road trip into the Texas hill country. He was like a wide-eyed kid, head turning this way and that to take in the vistas as they rolled toward the Frio River, seventy-five miles west of San Antonio, where Lu had found a perfect retreat. Too excited to realize he was tired, Dave never lay on the downy bed Lu had built, but they were able to pull over when he needed to empty one of his ostomy bags or walk a bit to relieve pressure from the ever-growing tumor and pain in his pelvis.

Once at the river, they planted chairs in the crystal waters of the Frio to cool their feet and refresh themselves in the late-summer Texas heat. Doctors had warned Dave that swimming was off limits; the bacteria could too easily cause a whole-body infection with his compromised immune system and open skin wounds. For days they sat and talked and talked "about everything" so that they knew one another's hearts inside and out. On their final day, Dave turned to Lu and said, "Do you think it will hurt me to lie down in the water? If I shower immediately afterward, do you think that would be OK?"

Lu didn't have to think it over before responding, "I think it'll hurt you if you *don't!*" With that, he threw caution to the wind and gave himself over to one last, glorious moment of surrender into his beloved Texas waters. Immersed in the precious moment, Dave spread his arms wide until his body lay like a cross with fresh, clear waters rushing over him. As if in baptism, he gave himself over to complete ecstasy. Lu watched her brother's face shimmer with joy as hers shined in a stream of tears, loss wrapped in gratitude and infinite love.

Wholehearted Love

After that expansive moment, Lu was visited with an extraordinary idea, "What if we came back here with the rest of our siblings? Just the brothers and sisters, no spouses and no kids!"

My shrine beside Spanish Creek at Oakland Feather River Camp
Dave soaking up the vibes of The Frio

Dave's face took on a faraway look, and then he answered, "Do you think they would come?"

The trademark Lu response was, "Well, we can ask." On fire to make it happen when she got home, she reached out to Perry, Jack, Jodee, and Randy. From one to the next, the answer was, without hesitation, "Yes!" Dave almost couldn't believe it, but he understood that it reflected the essential truth: he was wholeheartedly loved by each of his siblings. With planning underway for the Akard clan's Return to the Frio in early October, Dave, meanwhile, asked for a reunion of the Triumvirate. He reminded us that Lois's spirit was still very much present in their home, and by visiting, we would celebrate our mutual love for her. I'd just returned home from camp, but Sal and I were both compelled to say yes. Well aware of his shortening lifeline, Dave wanted us—as Lo's blood sisters—to help him with some decisions, like what to do with her journals and her ashes, and in mid-September, we made it happen. The new Triumvirate was in agreement: Lo's journals would be ceremonially burned to preserve her privacy. We waited until dark, then made a fire in the backyard pit where we slowly tore page after page, silently watching them burn. I only looked at her words once, astounded that my eyes landed on Lo's long-ago dream of searching in snow, descending in quicksand, and her disembodied spirit gazing down at the blue lake from above. I felt a shiver work its way up my body as the uncanny coincidence sparkled in my heart. Fertilizing the native plants in their yard with her ashes was a perfect honorarium to her values, and we carried it out the following afternoon, each of us wandering through their gardens and wild spaces while absorbed in private thoughts, ending in a Triumvirate-style hug in the front yard. Dave also organized a tree-planting ceremony at Westcave Preserve, planting a redbud tree in Lo's honor with the hope that the heart-shaped leaves would bring "broad Lois-type smiles" to many faces. Sal and I could see that, in taking those actions, Dave was readying himself for the transition that Lois had already made.

But before that could happen, a Return to the Frio with his five siblings would bring Dave into the acceptance and healing he'd longed for with his brothers. Once convened at the river, Dave's stamina was so challenged that he spent much of his time resting in bed, which gave each brother and sister quality one-on-one time with him as they wandered in and out of his room. Randy, the nurse, gave him the utmost quality of loving care-giving, and when he could rally, Dave joined the others around the dinner table. But the pièce de résistance was when he called everyone to the balcony and asked them, in his best counselor's roundabout way, to share stories. Jodee reminded them of drunkenly sneaking into the house past curfew and being met face to face by a wide awake mother, who, the next day demanded hung-over hedge trimming. This got them wandering further into teen-year territory and stories of adolescent acting out. The two older brothers were gruff, holding back at first and then finally confessed to a sin or two as the evening drew to a close. It was that very humanness, even their resistance to opening up, which opened Dave's heart to them. He forgave them for limitations that he'd previously taken as personal assaults. Acceptance replaced judgments until, like Lois and I, Dave found release from any lingering resentments with each of his siblings before he left this earthly plane.

Transitions

By Thanksgiving, Dave's balance was challenged, his breath short, and his energy waning. Still, he chanted and drove the long miles to Wimberley each week. When chatting by cell phone with his friend Sherry during one such journey, she was appalled, saying "Are you driving?" His answer was, "I ain't walkin', sister!" Dave drank and drank from the well of life until his belly was full. Even when it appeared that he would be too sick to make a planned trip to Oklahoma for Thanksgiving, he changed his mind at the last minute and decided to risk it. He got himself to the airport on Thanksgiving Day and showed up at his family gathering, bringing surprise and delight to the gathered clan around the food-laden table. He loved it. They loved it. And it took its toll.

Just before Christmas, a trip to the emergency room revealed how much the cancer had spread throughout his chest. Armed with an oxygen tank, he returned home but knew his time was near, and sent a beautiful good-bye e-mail, telling us, "The final stretch has begun, at least from the end of this physical form as I've known it, into the transition to the spiritual one that has always been waiting for me (for us all!). Even if we don't speak, please know that my love for each of you is just as strong and clear as ever. From my heart to all of your beautiful hearts, Dave." I needed to see him, needed one more chance to laugh, to tell him I loved him, and to say "Goodbye." So Seth and I headed to Austin, where Sally met us at the airport. Seth was coming down with a cold, so he stopped at the door and asked if it was OK to come in. Dave responded, "What's it gonna do, kill me?" We all laughed, and I thought, *He's accepted his death...he is waiting and willing.*

Goofy Goofing: Dave with Dr. Philip after a chant
Dave and Lo

His sisters Jodee and Lu were with him for the duration, grappling with his ups and downs. When he'd told Lu that he was ready for her to join him in Austin, that he needed her presence through the end, Jodee came too. Dave was beyond surprised, he was blown away when, without thinking a whit about it, Jodee loaded her car and drove all night from Tennessee to be at his side. The two sisters took care of Dave—and each other. For eight weeks, they left their lives behind and made Dave a number-one priority. But it wasn't easy. Like Lois, he wrestled with leaving the body he'd known for so long. He would let go, then try to take control, and then surrender again. He often cried easily and sweetly, wanting to relax into the care surrounding him as he lay on the couch in front of the crackling fire day after day. His pain tolerance was superhuman, but even he had met his match in lung cancer. True to his values of staying awake, he took only ten percent of the morphine allotted him. Lu told us that Dave was handling the process with great grace and strength, facing his situation head on, even with the bad days when he just didn't seem to be himself. Cantankerous when even his skin hurt from the eruptions on nearly every surface, Dave toughed it out, and though it was excruciating for Jodee and Lu, they honored his wishes, crying as they prepared meds, then putting on a smile when delivering the pills. Love and sorrow wound together as they held each other's hands through the stress of carrying out a vigil on a roller coaster.

There were great days, where they couldn't get him to rest if they duct taped him to the bed. He'd stand, oxygen tank at his side, chanting in ecstasy, then collapse in exhaustion as soon as his Siddha Yogi friends left. For Dave, the collapse was worth the ecstasy of God. But Lu and Jodee only felt the agony of watching him grapple with the ensuing pain. He often asked for his dinner to be re-heated five times, but barely took a bite. In spite of how much it hurt them to watch as Dave's body shut down, Lu said to the rest of the Akard sibs, "...you have no idea how grateful Jodee and I are that we're here, holding his hand and seeing the appreciation in David's eyes. He is soaking up the quiet and solitude in this process, knowing he has to go alone."

Kathy, the Overarching Angel, became an honorary sister to Jodee and Lu through the journey, often spending the night so they could actually sleep. She was there on the morning Dave died and told me the story of how he'd passed. Since cancer had spread through his lungs, breathing was becoming nearly impossible, and he struggled, wide-eyed, for breath, even as he refused the morphine that would relieve the gasping terror that came with the struggle. Finally, allowing just a little medication, he was able to relax, but without breath to speak, he simply gazed deeply into the eyes of his sisters, gently caressing their faces. Then he held his hands up in a T, as if to ask for a time-out. They stepped from the room, but a brief moment later, when Kathy peeked in, he was gone, his face turned toward the picture of his spiritual teacher, Gurumayi. It appeared as if he'd gazed at her while taking his final breath. Kathy told me, "Though it was disturbing to the rest of us, he passed in a state of wakefulness, dying just as he wanted to." I like to think that the T was Dave choosing his time, bursting consciously into his home beyond, the image of his spiritual guide as his gateway.

With Dave's death on the heels of losing Lois and my mother all in one year, I felt as if I had lived the twenty-third psalm, walking through the valley of the shadow of death. With one foot still in those lands, I sensed a transition of my own, a dying to my old self. Wanting to connect to their spirits, I paid a quiet visit to the rock cairns by Spanish Creek. The passing seasons had calmed the gushing waters so that small pools filled with fallen leaves formed where water had previously rushed. As I gazed over the waters, I thought of camp, of my family, and of the love I had poured out to each of them in the past years and was quite spontaneously filled with gratitude and a sense of completion. Though camp season number three had gone exceptionally well and relations with the CIC board were restored to positivity, I'd often described my experience as a salmon swimming upstream, pushing against the current. For over three years, I swam my heart out, but as I gazed into the softening waters, I realized I'd finally made it to the shallows—I'd become the kind of leader I wanted to be. Insight came to me in a flash; having arrived at the spawning ground, I was done. With caregiving for my family members behind me and eggs laid for a new life cycle at camp, I could stop swimming so hard. From Dave and Lois, I sensed an emotional blessing as it dawned on me that it was time to leave camp behind and take a great leap into the void.

EIGHT

Ancestor Speaking

Tonight I was feeling a little lost and looked at the photo of Lois on my refrigerator. I started talking to it, asking her, "What is life? What is death?" I said, "I don't understand existence." I made the Lo gesture of kissing her fingertips and throwing out her arms in thanks to the universe. I asked her to give me a sign.

As I spread my arms, the power in the house went off. The lights went dark, and the fan stopped spinning, just for a few seconds, and then lights, fan, air-conditioner, and compressor began again. All was dark for a few seconds and then sprang back to life as the digital clocks flashed their frozen time.

There was no weather, no reason for the power to go off. I had asked for a sign and was immediately given one. Still, my rational mind tried to find a reasonable cause.

I looked at Lois's picture. She seemed to be laughing. I still don't know what existence is, but Spirit is something that no one destroys. Like she said, "Love is all that matters."

—*Philip Riffe*
(Dave and Lo's longtime friend)

183

The Frozen Waterfall

As I mourned, I began to return my attention to home and hearth. That's when I realized how deeply my marriage needed to be fed. Seth understood what I'd been going through, having lost Cynthia to cancer, then his father a few years later. He knew how important it had been for me to be there for my family, understanding and upholding the vow I'd made with the Triumvirate. He'd been a supportive husband, gracefully accepting long absences as I came and went—to Baltimore, Austin, and camp. Though he was sympathetic, his needs had gone unmet for years. While he'd supported me through loss after loss, spending untold hours on the phone listening to frustrated tears, I'd been too absorbed to show him the same empathy. I'd been barely aware of how alone he felt or that he'd been struggling with big life questions of his own. I realized that if our union was to thrive, I needed to tend the garden of Seth. It was time to water our marriage with the same attention I'd given to everything else. We arranged to spend a long weekend at a beautiful inn nestled into the hills above the tiny fishing village of Marshall, where we savored the luxury of uninterrupted time in a suite overlooking Bodega Bay. We lay in the downy comfort of a white duvet, with white walls framing the windswept junipers out our window. The scent of salt and pinion was a backdrop to the pristine décor, which provided a blank canvas for painting a new story. We slept, read, and cozied up to one another; we lounged, and I told him I was ready to put him first. We talked about post-camp possibilities and about how to revitalize our relationship. We fantasized about sharing a retreat month in Italy, Costa Rica, or New Zealand, along with considering a yearlong soul immersion program that we'd each independently discovered. When we'd married, Seth and I set an intention that our union would be devoted to fulfilling our souls' purpose, both as a couple and as individuals. We'd chosen a *Ketubah* (a Jewish marriage contract) with an image of two trees standing side by side, with branches and roots intertwined. A portion of the contract reads, "May we remain committed to each other's physical and mental well-being and to each other's emotional and spiritual growth. May we always encourage and challenge one another to become the persons we are yet to be." In this spirit, we agreed that, while a month vacation sounded divine, being guided together in soul work was our deeper truth. We imagined that entering the yearlong program would help both of us connect to new possibilities, as well as deepen our bond and strengthen our individual roots, just like the trees on our Ketubah. Once the decision was clear, we set about with preparations, gathering camping equipment, writing in our journals more frequently, and opening up to our dreams. The night before the program started, I had a potent one:

I am leaving a small rural house filled with all my female relatives. Lois is with me, and we get into a car. She is driving, and soon we are sliding on a light layer of snow. We skid past a small cabin, and crash through the ice of a blue lake. To the left I see a beautiful, crystalline, frozen waterfall.

As we sink into freezing waters, I am frantically ripping off my seat belt and yelling at Lois to do the same. I have to save her because she is not saving herself, and I am terrified that she will die.

She slowly turns to face me with incredible stillness, gazing into my eyes with the most profound and abiding sense of peace. I feel she is saying, without words, that all is well.

When I woke, I felt Lois's presence, as if, more than a dream, I'd experienced a visitation. Feeling embraced by her peaceful gaze, I wept sweetly as I replayed the dream, taking in her piercing love and feeling she had brought me a message of grace. *That little cabin! It was just like the one at the Magothy!* Unraveling the dream images, I realized the crystalline waterfall reminded me of a photo I'd taken of Mom years before. It shows an exuberant Margie with her arms thrown to the heavens, celebrating the awe she felt at the magnificent frozen waterfall behind her. I thought about Lois's blue-lake dream and her blue-pearl association of spiritual ascendance. I contemplated the dive into the chilly waters as an underworld journey into the frozen aspects of my deep psyche. And I noted the feminine—even matriarchal—presence of my family. But I didn't want to work this dream in my ordinary way of sorting out the symbols and meanings. I just wanted to relish Lois's penetrating gaze. I felt an abiding trust that I was on the right path, diving into a watery underworld, guided by my Big Sister.

Visitation on the Snake River

The yearlong program, *Cultivating Soul-Infused Artistry and Leadership in a Time of Global Change*, began in Moose, Wyoming, at The Murie Center, the homestead of the Muries, longtime advocates for wilderness. Seth and I headed there, to the edge of Yellowstone Park, where notable figures such as John Muir and Teddy Roosevelt had held salons, discussing how to preserve the vast beauty of the natural world. Since the Murie's Homestead was bequeathed to The National Park Service and is reserved only for nature-awareness groups, we saw no humans outside of our group. Nestled into the cozy cabins along the Snake River, we did, however, frequently cross paths with elk, moose, bear, and deer. We fell into a kind of Aboriginal dreamtime, where the lines between the ordinary world and the right-brained, no-thought, animal body of our souls began to blur. It was there that I experienced a visitation from my ancestors. Even in my wildest dreams I could not have imagined I would experience an ancestral presence that I would call real. But it was a visceral experience of my family's presence, and to tell you the truth, it blew my mind! Following instructions from our guides, I was wandering solo on the land, consciously entering into the imaginal realm of the right brain when I stepped across a fallen, moss-covered log. As I straddled the log, a symbolic threshold between the worlds, I told myself, *I am now entering into the dreamtime.* I invoked the presence of my ancestors, unsure of who, if anyone, would show up. I encountered a gaggle of grouse, then wandered on, stopping dead in my tracks when I realized I'd been having an inner conversation with my Great-Aunt Myrtle for at least five minutes. *She's here!* I thought. Aunt Myrtle is my mother's aunt, part of my maternal clan, the Seidenman's. I'd spent my sixteenth summer working at her summer day camp, Camp Deer Creek, in the rounded mountainsides near Pittsburgh, where, on many a summer evening, we sat together on the sun-porch overlooking her wooded back yard. I'd sip Harvey's Bristol Creme Sherry from a tiny glass and luxuriate in the sweet, syrupy flavor of adulthood. That was more than forty years ago; if I'd expected anyone, it certainly wasn't her! Aunt Myrtle and I walked and talked as I clambered onto a sandbar, like a four-legged creature, until I found a warm spot where I could gaze onto the wide Snake River, its ripples reflecting the sun like tiny stars glistening over its surface. Looking into the sparkles, a wavy light formed in the air before me as my maternal clan gathered—a shimmering, almost visible collection of aunts, a few uncles, and a grandfather I'd never met—the space vitally alive. When I asked Aunt Myrtle why she had come, she said, "Our clan has been honoring the natural world for generations. I'm here to tell you that *beauty*, as an end unto itself, is enough." I responded by telling her about leaving camp, that I stood at a crossroads, and that I felt lost without Lois, uncertain of who I was in the world. She reassured me, "My dear, you made the right choice; you had to leave because you'll *never* change that patriarchal system! You will know what to do when the time is right. For now, just trust that beauty is enough. You mustn't worry about money; we have your back." With that, I felt each ancestor move through my body from back to front—like shadow bodies marching through my solar plexus with more substance than smoke but less than water. I felt my body literally being touched, as when my father's spirit had hugged me good-bye one last time. It was so powerful that, for most of the conversation, I'd been weeping. I asked her if they were my tears or hers, and she said, "Oh no, my dear, they are *all* of our tears." She went on to speak about the love of the earth that we Seidenman's share, the importance of caring for what we love, and then ended by reminding me that the earth is made of the same substance as humans. I was awed. Dumbfounded, really. She then comforted me by saying, "There is a place in the world that is calling to you, that needs you, but be patient. Don't move too fast or try to figure it out just yet. Trust that you have a mission ahead. It involves the rainbow bridge." Stunned, I began to furiously write in my journal lest I forget any tidbit. I wrote that although the Seidenman clan appeared gentle, I needed to recognize the tremendous strength of my matriarchal lineage. Aunt Myrtle reassured me that they were there, supporting me, loving me, and urging me forward.

I wanted to absorb the power of this visit, so with thoughts bouncing through my delighted but boggled mind, I jumped over a creek and re-crossed the threshold, landing back in ordinary reality. I entered a large meadow surrounded by a circle of massively tall ponderosa pines, where I sat quietly with my lunch, chewing slowly, reverently receiving the nourishment and considering what had just happened. Though I dismissed her comment about a rainbow bridge, thinking it sounded awfully woo-woo, I pondered, *If people fall in love with the beauty and splendor of the earth, will that mean they will begin to care for her?* I wondered if that was the mission that lay before me.

As if that wasn't enough for one day, I was startled when, abruptly, I felt my parents' presence bursting through the veil between worlds. In order to fully greet them, I tucked away my lunch, then stepped across a hastily drawn threshold, back into the dreamtime. I was immediately drawn into a group hug. Mom,

Lois, and Dad were there, as real as the entire clan I'd just left at the river. Their spirit arms embraced me as I cried tears of joy. I stepped back as they shifted from jubilant reunion to ceremonial preparation. Mom stood front and center, Dad to her left, and Lois to her right, each of them in their most vibrant spirit bodies, no sign of old age or cancer on any of them. I thought, *This is odd; Dad would never, ever NOT be in the lead!* Then my mother, dressed in her favorite flowered blouse, held up a sparkling diamond-studded crown and placed it on my head, saying, "You are carrying the matriarchal lineage now. I pass this honor to you. You must carry it with grace." I felt a tingling sensation in my scalp as the tiara energetically melted into and through the top of my head, the crown, also known as the seventh chakra. I understood that this was no ordinary imagination; I was being taken through a rite of passage, what Earth-centered traditions call a Croning or Eldering Ceremony. I was to carry the acquired wisdom of my mother's lineage, a passage which would require me to carry *beauty* into the world, just as Aunt Myrtle had prophesied. In a ceremonial tone, Mom said, "You are beautiful." Then Dad, a bit out of focus in the background, simply said, "I am proud of you." Lois, dressed in a peasant skirt with the long wavy black hair of her youth, repeated again and again, "You can do it…" followed by, "I trust you…" as she handed me a sheaf of papers. "I give you permission to use these any way you want. It's up to you to carry on my work." I'd been given the responsibility for carrying out the work of my matriarchal lineage. A tangle of emotions swirled as I felt both the honor and the weight of these beautiful tasks laid on my shoulders.

Seidenman Clan (Mom is the dark haired beauty on the bottom right)
Aunt Myrtle
My maternal grandparents: Mommy Helen and Daddy Lou
Mom celebrating life and beauty at the frozen waterfall

Return to Circle

Back in the circle, we shared stories of ancestral visitations. Realizing what matriarchal eldership would require of me, I asked the tribe to call me by a new name: "Grace," hoping it would help me live up to and embody the quality. Then, riveted, I listened to their stories of tailors, miners, and warriors. I was especially moved when Seth told a tale of his grandfather astride a camel, fighting for Israel's statehood. As he wondered at the vision, I saw clearly how that ancestral value was alive and well in my husband's heart. His longtime work for social justice, supporting the disenfranchised and building community through collaboration among otherwise disconnected groups, made all the more sense to me as I saw how deeply it was woven in his ancestral lineage. *What a beautiful soul he is,* I thought. We stood back to back, supporting one another as we leaned into our ancestral energies. In solidarity, we sorted the gathered clues and watched one another in wonder.

With Lois's creative environmental work, Aunt Myrtle's reinforcement of our clan's connection to the beauty of nature, and with my recent work at camp, I'd first imagined that Lois had transmitted the nature-immersion camp curriculum for city youth she'd written a few years before. I felt honored that she would entrust her work into my hands. But soon, thoughts about completing Lois and Dave's book project took root. That's when I realized that Lois had passed something way more precious to me than the El Ranchito camp curriculum. On that day, beside the Snake River, Lois had entrusted her most deeply valued and intimate story, *Two Rare Birds*, into my care.

Signs of Spirit

Lois and Dave had long talked of writing about their experiences of cancer and the blessing of love and spirit which grew out of their journey. Now that both of them were gone, the project seemed to start writing itself—chapter titles and phrases coming through me but not from me. *Joy in the middle. See you on the other side. Love is all that matters.*

Dave's memorial service was scheduled to be in Austin, and as I drove there, the road trip became a pilgrimage in which I'd awaken each morning with words tumbling from my mind, flowing so fast that I rushed to my computer where pages poured out; I was simply the vehicle, listening to and capturing Lois and Dave's words. The ease with which *Two Rare Birds* flowed from my fingers felt like a sign that I was supposed to carry out their mission. *Am I doing this for them or for me?* I wondered. *Maybe both,* I heard in my head.

Dave's memorial was held at Ruby Ranch, a retreat center in the rolling hills just outside of Buda. Among many eulogies, Dave's longtime friend, Philip Riffe (as distinct from Dr. Philip), told us how he'd sat with Dave near the end, when Dave had asked, "I want to know if it's all right if I contact you after I'm gone." Philip had responded with, "I wanted to ask if you would." Then Dave said, "I only ask that you don't put any restrictions on it. Be open to anything. It could come from anywhere." Dave loved to sing, so it was natural that the ceremony closed with a chant, after which we sat in receptive silence. Then, on that windless afternoon, the back door of the chapel slowly creaked open, then slammed firmly shut. Dave's words, "Don't put any restrictions on it. It could come from anywhere," reverberated through the sanctuary. Our stunned eyes popped open as we looked back and forth at one another, then all burst into laughter and applause. It seemed that, like Elvis, Dave had left the building.

Ashes to Ashes

Since Sally and I were together for the memorial, we saw it as an opportunity to finally spread Mom's ashes. It was wildflower season in Texas, and Mom's love of flowers made for perfect timing. With ashes stowed alongside a packed lunch, we headed toward Pedernales Falls State Park in the Texas hill country. Lo and Dave had taken each of us there to enjoy clear waters cascading over limestone and through the wide channel filled with gullies and gorges; we agreed it was an ideal spot to perform our ceremony. We scrambled over the soft rock and hopped over mini-waterfalls and eddies until we found a secluded, five-foot waterfall spilling into a small pool. Surrounded by the privacy of ten-foot, white boulders, we invoked sacred space by burning sage. I offered up a prayer: "As we release Mom's ashes, let it be a release for us also. May the wounds of our ancestral clans and any limitations that keep us from expressing our truest purpose, be released into these ashes as they return to the water and the earth." Sally continued, "We release ourselves from our stuck places and our grief. And we ask for support from the invisible forces of life to help us in these intentions." Then, little by little, we started shyly dropping small handfuls of Mom into the river. Tiny pieces of bone sank to the base of the riverbed while lighter ashes flew into the air. Some swirled in spirals, catching the current of the river. We watched, then became more bold, tossing larger and larger handfuls into the precious water. When all of the ashes were gone, we sat silently for a long time before moving to close the ceremony. Just then, a young family sprang over the boulders, and we smiled, agreeing telepathically that the cycle of rebirth and renewal had begun.

Later that night, our last evening together, Sally and I sank into Lois and Dave's couch with companionable ease. We'd said good-bye to our people, leaving big spaces hollowed out of our chests, which neither of us felt compelled to fill. I was surprised then, when I heard a gasp and Sally burst out with, "I've just had an idea!" And before I could reply, "But I'm afraid to say it out loud."

"C'mon, Sal, be brave!" Whatever it was, I knew she'd tell me.

She said, "What if we start a foundation in their honor? I bet this is just how the Susan B. Komen Foundation was formed... sisters sitting around after saying good-bye to the one who'd died from breast cancer." Then, suddenly animated, we looked at each other and, in unison, said, "We could do it!" We were two birds in a nest beginning to rise like phoenixes from our mother's—and sister's—ashes.

Red Mesa

A week later, I left Austin and headed to New Mexico to visit my friend Stephen, who was steward of a piece of land west of Albuquerque called Red Mesa. When I discovered that Red Mesa was an outlying village, of which Chaco Canyon is the heart, I got really excited. Chaco Canyon is soul home for me. It is known as the ceremonial epicenter of the Anasazi people, where massive buildings (now preserved ruins) give testimony to the engineering acumen of the Pueblo people. As the hub of a huge wheel of sacred geometry, from the center place of Pueblo Bonito, a complex road system stretches outward in all directions to outlying communities. The roads from Pueblo Bonito create an image of a wheel, an archetypal symbol for the cycle of life, when seen from above.

Chaco is located in the northwest corner of New Mexico; the closest town is Farmington, which is pretty much in the middle of nowhere. I've been there five times, turning off the paved road at the shuttered gas station for the forty-five minute dusty drive through a vast, high desert of sagebrush and scrub juniper. With no services other than a visitor center and campground, it is brightly still in the day and dark black, save for starlight, in the night. Hiking through narrow cataracts of rock, only to emerge on mesas overlooking the ruins of a once-vital civilization, is eerily inspiring. These canyons are filled with shell fossils, ancient petroglyphs, and the remaining clay-brick structures which are dotted with underground ceremonial chambers called *kivas*. In the distance is Fajada Butte, where a complex calendar is formed by spirals carved high on the red rock behind perfectly placed several-ton boulders. A band of sunlight, referred to as a sun dagger, passes through the boulders, piercing the center of the petroglyph to mark summer and winter solstices. Two sun daggers frame the edges of the spiral on spring and fall equinoxes. In another play of light and shadow, a nineteen-year lunar cycle is recorded when moonlight pierces another, smaller petroglyph spiral beside the solar marker. Clearly these ancient people carried wisdom and a great understanding of astronomy.

The Anasazi mapped the movement of the heavens onto the earth, spirit into matter, creating a powerful energy which I found beautiful and mystical. The first time I clambered up a steep cliff and stood next to a petroglyph, a nine-inch spiral carved into the side of a red-rock bluff, I felt an uncanny sense of déjà vu. My heart stirred, and I thought, *Someone from ancient times made that, and here I am touching it, too.* I felt connected to something or someone from another world, as if by invisible threads. To this day, anytime I encounter ancient markings from an earlier culture, I feel as if ancestors are speaking to my heart.

Stephen and I pulled into crusty Red Mesa just as a sweat-lodge ceremony was about to begin. A sweat lodge is a Native American ceremony of spiritual and physical cleansing. Hot like a sauna but enacted with sacred ceremony, stepping into the lodge is symbolic of entering the womb of Mother Earth. By accepting the fortuitous invitation to join the sacred sweat at Red Mesa, I knew I would shed some layers and hopefully emerge reborn. Without much time to prepare, I wrapped into a sarong and crawled into the hut, settling onto the dirt floor for whatever would unfold. The hot rocks were ceremonially brought into the lodge, aroma wafting from the sage and sweetgrass sprinkled on each as it was lovingly placed in the center of our womb. Then the flap was closed; it was completely dark—so dark I couldn't see my hand in front of my eyes. I embraced that privacy and waited for the heat to overtake me. There were four rounds to the ceremony, each with prayer and song, giving us four opportunities to shed what needed to be shed. I felt my muscles melting and layers of grief stored in my body sweating out of my pores. During the final round, we were invited to offer up prayers for the world. I was astounded to hear myself say, "As humans, we are privileged to have the opportunity to serve Spirit. Being embodied is a great honor, for it is through the matter of our physical beings that we are able to serve Life. For this I give great and humble gratitude." Lois and Dave, through their deaths, had shown me the preciousness of life. Losing them solidified a commitment: I would *not* take my life for granted.

Rainbow Bridge

Red Mesa, like Chaco, had gotten under my skin, and I began wandering there, much as I had on the retreat in Wyoming. I found a shady spot, where I sat with my back against the terra-cotta rock at the base of a huge bluff. I introduced myself to the massive mesa and learned her name: Red Bluff. Then I laid my body down on her. I asked if there was anything she wanted to say to me. She told me, "Rocks are the bones of the earth. All rocks are connected through the lava at the center of the earth, and no matter what type—whether they live in desert, river, or ocean—they are all part of the skeleton of the Earth. When we touch one boulder, we touch the entire Earth." Later I shared this with Leland, the Navajo shepherd who cared for the rare strain of sheep at Red Mesa. He answered, "Yes, this is what my people believe."

I'd also asked Red Bluff, "What is the connection between Chaco and Red Mesa? What is my connection with the Anasazi? Why am I called to these places?" She told me, "The Anasazi are not of this place. They were sent here on a mission to build a Rainbow Bridge. You've been called here to Red Mesa and Chaco because you are of the Anasazi clan, not of their bloodline but of their spirit line. You are part of creating the Rainbow Bridge once again." The words resonated.

Truth had been delivered. I felt as if I'd sat in front of the Dalai Lama, who'd transmitted the meaning of my existence. I remembered how I'd dismissed Aunt Myrtle's mention of a rainbow bridge. I thought, *Too woo-woo, indeed, Lily Grace. Time to wake up and listen!*

On my way back to the Red Mesa ranch house, I found Chacoan pot chards in a dry streambed. When I held them in my hands, I felt just as I had when touching the ancient spiral petroglyph, as if I were linked by invisible threads to the people who had made those pots centuries ago. When I shared my story with Leland, the Navajo shepherd, he told me he'd seen a petroglyph of the Rainbow Bridge about a half-hour hike from there. An hour later, we stood before a wall of petroglyphs chipped into the red rock. Amid spirals, bighorn sheep, human figures, and antelope, a rainbow, bridging the fingertips of two hands, was before me. *No small accident*, I thought as I stood in awe before that carved Rainbow Bridge.

I'd read that handprint petroglyphs carried messages from one shaman to another. Seth and I had experimented with this at Chaco and had received unique and distinct messages each time we placed our hands on what we called the Shaman's Hand. In years hence, I'd introduced it to pilgrimage participants, and it never failed to teach a lesson or deliver a timely message. I became very still, then reached up and placed my hands on the two hands of the petroglyph. I could only do this by leaning against the bluff and raising both arms straight up over my head. My hands fit perfectly into the indentations in the rock, and I waited, but received no visionary message. Surprised that I felt nothing, I thought maybe I was doing it wrong, pulled back, and made an offering of water to the spirits of the place. I settled some more and tried again. Still there was nothing, but as I listened more intently, I recognized a feeling so familiar, so known, so *home* that I hadn't noted it as anything unusual. As I tuned in more fully to this home feeling, I felt as if I was merging with the bluff's heart, deeply comforted. It came to me: *New Mexico is the home of my spirit.*

Giant Butterfly

As Lois continued to reveal herself to me in dreams and visions, my trust in the other side—the invisible reality that lay behind the curtain of daily life—grew. When the one-year anniversary of Lo's passing approached, I dreamed that Sal, Lo, Dave, and I were standing before a claw-foot bathtub with water pouring into it and flowing over the sides. A magnificent, bigger-than-life multicolored butterfly emerged from the waters. Lois turned and gazed into my eyes in the same, wordless way she had in the frozen-waterfall dream, as if to say, "This is one HUGE transformation!" Butterflies represent new life born from the old, emerging from a cocoon in which a caterpillar had become mush before growing into a new being. I woke up thinking, *The ice has melted, and I am coming into a new form!* Floating in the cleansing waters of the dream, I began to swim toward a new connection with my maternal ancestral clan.

My paternal line was still strong within me, but the forceful energies of Pop-Pop and his persecution complexes were giving way to acceptance and the warm, gentle joy of the Seidenman clan. Beauty started carrying more weight than achievement. Until now, I'd been living a patriarchal lineage, valuing doing over being, but that was shifting. As

I changed, so did my relationships; some fell away and others strengthened. I became more compassionate toward my own failures and others' fallibilities. The changes weren't, and still aren't, without effort. But as I practiced graceful forgiveness toward others and myself, I couldn't help but wonder, *Was this completing the clan wave?*

Crying for a Vision

Seth and I had been to two of the four retreats in our yearlong program, and our marriage had been well fed. We were growing closer as our honest self-reflection and vulnerability muscles grew. We'd spent an entire week doing shadow work, which meant that we uncovered aspects of ourselves that had previously been hidden in the unconscious. Among other sub-personalities, I discovered my inner torchbearer, who, like my father, was dedicated to the good, the right, and the honorable fight. I imagined her much like the Olympiad runner, her golden, shimmering body sprinting to right the wrongs of the world. I discovered that she did this without regard to her impact, and as I began to understand my deeply ingrained pattern of overshadowing others with righteous certainty, I awakened a new openness, making room for truths beyond my own. I softened. Seth, too, did his work and I watched him unfold to his inner beauty, something others saw but he'd previously missed. On the way to each retreat, we sang or sat quietly, occasionally sharing our intentions for the upcoming workshop. On the way home, we took turns reading our most private revelations to one another from our journals. As we witnessed each other's soul work on wild lands and spent hours in the car, driving to and from the wild red rocks of Utah's Capitol Reef or Canyonlands, intimacy grew between us as we released one another from expectations of perfection and accepted the shadows of our love.

We were midway through the yearlong soul immersion when our tribe gathered for a vision fast—an ancient initiatory rite carried out by indigenous people the world over. We each would be fasting for four days, drinking only water and living alone in the wilderness. It was the perfect opportunity to explore my surfacing questions: *What am I supposed to do now? Is* Two Rare Birds *part of it? What IS the Rainbow Bridge? Am I supposed to start a nonprofit of some kind?* During the fast, I would send my questions, as a lament, into the wild. I felt ready to understand my purpose and restore my sense of place in the world. Although I'd begun work on *Two Rare Birds*, its form wasn't entirely clear. Sally's idea for a foundation was planted in my imagination, but I couldn't see its mission. I had been given two directives about a rainbow bridge, but without understanding what it was, how could I build it? Messages about beauty and the preciousness of being embodied was all a big swirl in my head. I was still in the dark, trying to piece the puzzle of me back together. In other words, I was completely ripe for a vision fast.

With excitement and trepidation, I lifted my backpack and walked into the forest, hoping to receive a vision during this extended dreamtime. Though I was ultimately going solo, I was not entirely alone as I wandered beside another woman, my buddy, who'd asked to be called "River," along the canyon's edge. Trudging through tangles of scrub oak and past tall trunks of burned-out junipers, each of us sought a power spot for our quest. River found hers first, in a glade of soft grasses, and I found mine soon after, perched on a bluff at the edge of the canyon. I knew it was my spot the minute I spied the red-rock outcropping through the bush then, heart beating double-time, scrambled the twenty-five feet down a small, winding trail onto the wide ledge to claim it as my own. We then found a clearing halfway between us, where we created a small circle of rocks, agreeing to meet there at daybreak on the final morning of our solo. Until then, it would serve as a safety net. Each morning, I would place a smooth round rock into my side of the circle (sometimes adding a flower); every afternoon River moved it into hers, often with a sweet note. If either of us found the rock unmoved, it was a sign to immediately check on the others' well-being.

With the circle built, we made offerings, spoke prayers, hugged, then silently bid one another adieu. I returned to my spot, where I felt deeply free of human company, surrounded by red sandstone and white granite. A row of immense ponderosa pines lay to the north, as recognizable to me as family from my forays at camp and by the Snake River. Behind me, to the east, rose a cliff-like face of sprawling juniper and scrub oak. In the south, an oak tree, large enough for shade, bordered my spot and a red-rock promontory reached out over the canyon to the west. In the center of all that beauty, I gave a huge sigh of gratitude, then set about ceremonially building cairns in each of the directions. I moved slowly, stopping often for water or shade. Every action was sacred; I blessed every rock used to build the cairns, which set boundaries around my sacred space. As I stacked the rocks one upon the other, I prayed to be given wisdom from the north, inspiration from the east, openness from the south, and introspection from the west. I returned to the soft-sand center each time I completed a cairn, as if it were the heart of my circle. Twenty-five feet in diameter, I felt deeply safe inside the space I'd created. For now, it was my home and my temple. When I placed my camp chair in the yielding sand, I felt as if I were the hub of the wheel of my own sacred geometry, much like the ceremonial chambers of Pueblo Bonito in Chaco Canyon. With a contented sigh, I relished the resounding silence of the canyon as exquisite grace. I carefully placed my sleep mat and bag beside my chair and journal. There, I waited.

As night fell, I curled into my sleeping bag beneath a bright blanket of stars. Having fasted for two days, I fell easily into rest. Just before drifting into sleep, I shouted into the canyon, "Is *Two Rare Birds* my next endeavor?" I was hoping for a dream to guide me. But it was a deep, dreamless sleep until morning's first blush, when I was surprised awake by a fluttering sound. I peeked from my sleeping bag to find a tiny, bright-yellow goldfinch in a bush inches from my head. As I carefully turned to see her more closely, she startled, and then flew into a towering ponderosa. I sat up to greet the day, feeling as if the bright-yellow finch had been a good omen, a colorful awakening into my first solo morning. Suddenly, two evening grosbeaks, brightly colored black and yellow birds four times the size of the goldfinch, burst from the massive pines. They chased one another playfully, first in one direction, then the other, circling the trees this way and that. As suddenly as they'd appeared, they vanished into the jumble of dark branches. Silence. Then, tumbling together, head over wing, tail over beak, they fell from the tree entwined, plummeting toward the earth. I realized they were mating! They fluttered, separated, and then swooshed away together. The canyon returned to its prior stillness, and I, fully awakened by their display, moved into my day. Inordinately happy, I traveled the path to leave a message for River, rolling the rock into my side of our stone circle. Returning to my power spot, I was mid-scramble down the skinny trail when the same two grosbeaks burst from the trees. Again they performed their death-defying ritual, first playfully circling, then disappearing, and finally plunging toward the ground, mating. I watched in awe, then, as if struck by lightning, I thought, *TWO RARE BIRDS!* I suddenly remembered my question shouted into the wild world the night before, and in that millisecond, those two brightly colored birds flew off to the north, never to return again.

Dave had often spoken about birds being drawn to Lo. One of his stories popped to mind as I sat down, mid-trail, to reflect on the visitation. He'd brought Lo home from rehab, gone into the house for the wheelchair, and returned to ask, "Are you ready?" When she surprised him with, "No," he followed her pointing finger to see two red-tailed hawks mating in their front yard. I'd also learned from Lo's best birding buddy that mating birds were drawn to Lo, so that even when the two of them gazed into the same vista, only Lois could spot the feathered mating. Lois, my rare bird, and Dave, her equally rare mate, were speaking to me. When I thought how they had come TWICE, I laughed out loud into the canyon quiet, feeling silly for missing their first message. But the double visit doubly clarified it: *Two Rare Birds* was my next endeavor. Dave and Lois were flying free, guiding me toward my purpose! Humbled, my faith in the abiding presence of the invisible world was rooted ever deeper into the soil of me.

Day two had barely begun, and I felt as if I'd gotten what I came for—a big resounding *Yes!* As time passed, ever so slowly, I followed the sun, moving from place to place, tracking the light from sunrise to sunset. Moments of revelation were book ended by boredom and uncertainty, as I wondered if anything was really happening. I hungered for insight, turning over and over what I knew about rainbows, how they are revealed only when light streams through mist, making the invisible visible through color. Moving around my circle like a planet, I thought about rainbows as luminosity made real. If the sun, as the basis of all flora and fauna, is the source of all matter on earth, then light is its messenger. Light is the *substance* of which matter is formed. I thought, *Light is spirit embodied. We humans truly are made of stardust!* Slowly, it dawned on me that the rainbow bridge is a link between the invisible and visible worlds. *A rainbow is spirit in matter!* Insights started piling up, one on top of the other, like the rock cairns I'd built...*When?* It seemed like forever ago. I started understanding that just as light splits into color when refracted through a prism, spirit splits into the many faces of humanity. Just as light manifests as a multicolored rainbow, spirit manifests into a body as the multifaceted human being.

I started thinking about all the colors as fragmented, or wounded, aspects of myself—my inner hero and torchbearer, my wounded child and magical inner playmate. I thought about the loyal and righteous one who ensured justice and service, no matter the cost, and about the nurturing and generative adult inside of me. I began to see that all of them were different colors making up one whole rainbow of me.

As I sat in my circle, I felt whole, connected at the center by invisible, multicolored roads reaching out from my hub, each slice a fragment of my own brightly lit heart—the sun at the center of my being. I knew, also, that this went beyond my personal psyche. These infinite colors seemed to similarly represent the wider wounds of humanity. If we were not wounded, the light would not be split into a majesty of different aspects and forms of humanity. My mind reeled, but I could only absorb so much. I grabbed my colored pencils and started doodling. Phew! Without meaning to, I drew a rainbow pouring out of the sun, penetrating a heart, then grounding into the Earth. I saw that the human heart *is* the crystal, breaking open the multi-hued miracle of life in all its forms. Everything—and everyone—is part of life's multiplicity *and* singularity. We are *all* expressions of the rainbow bridge—spirit expressed through matter. I thought, *The rainbow bridge isn't a thing, it's a consciousness.* The rainbow bridge is symbolic of Oneness.

Only one question remained. I asked Lois and Dave, as if they were sitting with me in my sacred circle, whether they would support a nonprofit founded in their honor. Like a mirage, they materialized before me and answered, "As long as it's about the body and the Earth," came from Lois, and, "As long as it serves Spirit," from Dave. Then they disappeared. I thought, *Spirit into matter, and matter into spirit, perfect!* I felt a grand sense of purpose—*Two Rare Birds* was more than an expression of love for Lois and Dave, it was also something I was here on this planet to do.

Other revelations came and went. Soon it was time to greet River at our stone circle. We trudged back to base camp, three gallons of water lighter. Our tribe greeted us with drumming, howling, and hugs. Overcome, I wept for joy and for the beauty I'd left behind, smiling into the eyes of my fellow seekers, then falling into the familiar comfort of Seth's arms, curious about the visions he'd brought back from his solo. Together, we practically flew the nine hundred miles home, sharing every mundane detail of our visions, intent on carrying them out.

The Blue Pearl

Later that summer, traveling in Costa Rica for a friend's fiftieth birthday, I was still floating in the bubble of mystical awakenings. Devoted to *Two Rare Birds*, I'd written every day and found quiet places to meditate on what would come next. I'd become accustomed to calling upon Lois's spirit for guidance. Often she appeared, sometimes Dave was by her side, the ever-present transparent, wavy lines moving over the surface of their images. One day, peering over the rainforest treetops to the ocean beyond, I asked for help and was shocked when Lois said, "Lily, you have to let me go. It's time for me to move on." Though she spoke briskly, her voice was not without compassion. I realized her words were true, but I didn't want them to be. Trying to hold her close, I said, "But I need your help with the book." With a penetrating gaze, she spoke forcefully, saying, "I sacrificed my life so *you* could write this book. It's *yours* now. So, go *write it*!!" I couldn't believe what I was hearing. *Sacrificed?* I began to sob, sorrow mixed with guilt, remembering my vision from Seer—me standing over Lo bleeding with a spear through her heart. *She sacrificed her life so I could write this book?*

Scrambling for a foothold, I looked to Dave, asking, "What do you think?" With a lighthearted gesture, he crooked his thumb toward Lois and said, "I'm with her!" I was outnumbered. And in my heart, I knew they were right; I had to let her go.

My sobs turned to gentle weeping when a shimmering silver drop, like a bead of water, appeared in my imagination. It fell into my third eye, where I watched it slowly descend like the 1960s TV commercials for Pearl Shampoo. Lo and I had marveled at the long, slow journey the pearl took to reach the bottom of the bottle. Similarly, this vision moved in slow motion; it captured my full attention as the droplet fell into a pool the color of mercury. Ripples emanated out and out, while a deep peace came over me. My tears became droplets of acceptance, then gratitude, as the pearl's currents expanded. Lois instilled a truth into me: she and I had a soul contract. She had completed her part, and now I had to do mine. Acceptance replaced resistance as a deep feeling of wholeness and completion filled my being. I understood what it meant to have a shared mission and to carry it out together; Lois's death had been the ultimate act of service to our common purpose. I remembered the crackling vibration at my third eye, from the night before Lo's final surgery; it was as if it's pulsations had expanded my chakra all the way open. I realized: *Lois has sent me a transmission.*

When I wondered whether I'd experienced the state of transcendence known by spiritual seekers as the blue pearl, my curiosity was sated through the miracle of Google. I learned that, just like I'd seen, it is sometimes perceived as a silver drop at the third eye. I found that Swami Muktananda, the Siddha Yoga founder, had written, "Seeing it in meditation is like seeing the soul." *That's what I experienced in Costa Rica!* Inspired to dig deeper into Lo's communication, I looked up the word sacrifice and found that it came from the Latin roots *Sacer,* meaning "holy," and *facere,* meaning "to make holy." I began to accept that Lois's sacrifice was part and parcel of our holy, shared soul path. The revelation of the blue pearl showed me that everything that had happened was *supposed* to happen—and I mean *everything,* including Lo's cancer journey and our tumultuous relationship, which was the painful grist that had honed both Lo and I into more forgiving people. It gave me a newfound trust in destiny.

Nine

Legacy

Lois and Dave's journey propelled me deeper into the questioning of my true identity: pure consciousness, unchanging and eternal. I learned that when one truly lets go of the story, the surrender seats us in an ever deeper, profound stillness and peace—pure awareness.

We are not the story written on the paper, we are the pure-white paper itself. What can be more heavenly than resting in the depths of this peace, our true nature?

When our stories are over, we will not count the days. We will remember how deeply love flowed, the pleasure of our shared company, the peace. We will know it was perfect.

—Ellen

One Thread

Once Lois demanded that I make *Two Rare Birds* my own, the book took on a new shape. Chapter titles were changed, and big sections were cut. The arc of the story became mine, not theirs. I'd thought I was writing about Dave and Lo's transformation, but it was my own journey, intricately woven with Lois's, that I knew most intimately. I did what Lo asked of me; I let her go. As I rewrote page after page, I began to understand the long journey Lois and I had made from betrayal to forgiveness. The writing helped me rise out of the deep cold and dark waters of my dream as I wove our wounds and triumphs together into one vast tapestry. As if sitting at a loom, I gathered the threads of Lo's blue lake and my frozen one. They blended with strands of blue pearl, a multi-colored rainbow bridge, and vibrant ancestral visitations until the spirit fabric revealed that light is the connective tissue of all life. The more I wrote, the more I understood that rejecting the invisible world is like saying that because I cannot see it, air does not exist. I wrote myself into a new sense of Self, one strand amid infinite color, knitted in an exquisite, weightless web. Pull on any thread, and the whole pattern is changed, *because it's all one thread.*

Throughout the writing process, I've identified with Inanna, who was encouraged to visit Ereshkigal by Ninshubar, her trusted feminine servant, who, it turned out, eventually rescued her. Lois was *my* Ninshubar! She'd initiated me into the dark waters of my underworld psyche, where I came undone, but she also rescued me from them, awakening the grace and beauty of our maternal lineage and showing me how to trust in the infinite pattern of our souls' journey.

Though I miss her every day, I am grateful for the challenging path we have walked, leading me to this moment where I choose, moment by moment, to fulfill my part of our soul contract. It is my promise to her.

Completing the Clan Wave

Perched before the ancient tribal hearth, I have been surprised to find so many ancestors making an appearance. Their tangible presence, then absence, has left me wonder-struck with the knowledge that I am standing on the backs of all who have come before me. It could be no other way. We are part of one another's lives—and, therefore, part of each other's story. Sitting with Lois in her final hours (and at the bedside of Dave and my father) has become the fabric of my transformation. Meeting my grandfather and great-aunt in memory and vision has enlivened all my relations, even with ancestors whose names I do not know. I envision each of them having sat by the bedside of one who has come before her, and the one before him, all the way back through time, until I see that I am interwoven with each and every one who has attended that rite of passage. I feel their presence and the sacred power discovered at the threshold between worlds.

Inspired by my ancestors, I am living into what it means to complete my clan wave, merging my bloodlines as I embrace both my paternal and maternal lineages in equal measure. Lois's revelation of "love is all that matters" became mine too, and I feel her support from the other side, still helping me grow. She showed me that to identify only with Pop-Pop's story of persecution and immigration, or the strength that grew from that trauma, was to cut off an essential part of me. With her dream-world guidance, I have come to embrace the grace of my mother's lineage so that now my strength is tempered with beauty, tipping my scales toward balance in this sacred marriage of opposites.

Though *Two Rare Birds* has become my own story, in my heart it remains an homage to Lois and Dave's cancer journey. As they confronted death, love was passed back and forth until it circled around with no beginning or end. Love was the one thing, after all was said and done, that mattered. Because of that, I awakened to the power of forgiveness. I was able to say good-bye to Lois without remorse—a gift I will forever treasure. My losses have led me to accept that being born, living a life, and facing death are parts of one whole package. And the truth of what Lois said again and again, "This moment is all we have," is finally emblazoned permanently in my heart. Death, in all its terrible, heart-cracking, life-shattering ways has shown me that any day could be the last. No longer will I wait to love, to forgive, or to walk, as best I can, in beauty.

Spirit of Resh

As *Two Rare Birds* unfolded, every day I burned a bit of sage before sitting in meditation and only then did I put words to paper. Day by day, the writing has deepened and informed my journey.

Chapter by chapter, my belief that death is a sacred passage has strengthened. I wondered why dying was not as openly honored and celebrated as birth, and I began to think about how our culture treats it as a failure of the medical system, which is designed to promote life at all costs. It is seen as a betrayal of a youth-oriented, age-defying society that acts as if growing old should be hidden behind closed doors. As the rawness of my grief transformed into words on the page, a tender acceptance grew, and I realized that mourning is too often approached as something to just *get through*. Yet for me, death had been anything but a failure. Loss was the opposite of something to get past; it became the ultimate transformational opportunity. I realized, *No matter what has gone before, death offers a moment of truth in which anything can happen.* Beyond gratitude for the moments of truth between Lois and me, the realization that none of us will escape death became more real than ever. I thought, *What IS a failure is sweeping death under the rug.* Losing Lois and Dave had broken through my denial of mortality. It dawned on me that hiding death represses the heart and I felt a growing passion to bring it out of the closet.

One day, while immersed in errands, as I drove from the dog park to the grocery store, a phrase arose: *Helping people face death is a matter of soul and spirit.* As I drove, clarity grew until I knew with certainty that, frightening though it is, facing death informs life. They are intertwined forever, like an infinity symbol. The nonprofit would be devoted to awakening this truth. It would help people rediscover meaning—even purpose—in illness, death and in being alive, just as I had. This would be the grounding force of our nonprofit foundation. I had found my next calling.

Manifestation

With this clarity, I called Sally. We agreed that although the idea for a nonprofit had come from her, the vision and mission were coming through me now. The first phase of manifestation would be mine to carry. We searched for a name that would capture the essence of serving spirit and matter, just as Dave and Lo had expressed at my vision quest. We tossed words back and forth, none of them catching on. That's when, glancing at the framed Sun card on my bookshelf, chills ran up and down my entire body. Seeing the Hebrew letter at the bottom of the card, I said in a hushed rush, *"Resh!"*

After Sally's immediate, breathy response, "Yes!" what followed was months of legal forms, attorney e-mails, and nearly infinite red tape. At last, I completed the complex application to the IRS for the 501.c3 status that would make the Spirit of Resh Foundation a full-fledged, tax-exempt organization. It went to the post in late summer, and I settled in for a long wait. Summer passed into fall, and fall into winter as, like a pregnant mother-to-be, I waited for news from the IRS. Finally, in the New Year, on one sunny, Northern California day, I stopped at the bottom of my driveway. I told myself, *Today will be the day I hear from the IRS!* I reached into the black metal box and called on my inheritances, that patriarchal will and matriarchal strength. I whispered, "Please, Lo, make it happen! Make today the day!" Then, more fervently, "MAKE IT SO!" With fingers trembling and knees knocking, I closed my eyes and reached deep into the underworld. I sorted through the jumble of junk mail until I saw IRS emblazoned on an upper left corner. It was addressed to the Spirit of Resh Foundation.

Once inside, I took a deep breath, ceremoniously lifted the Italian letter opener, sliced the crease, and fished the paper from its cocoon. My eyes landed on the words, "We are pleased to inform you..." and I stopped reading. Bouncing around in circles like a puppy, I grabbed the phone, dialed Seth, and giggled my way through a chant: "It's a n-a-a--o-n-pro-fit! It's a n-a-a--o-n-pro-fit! We're a nonprofit!" Spirit of Resh Foundation, now a certified US-of-A nonprofit foundation and community-benefit organization, was born from the ashes of my grief.

Carrying On

The Foundation is living proof that, as surely as spring follows winter, out of death, new life is born. Several months after Spirit of Resh Foundation was fully incorporated, I had a big dream— the kind that sticks forever. It had startled me awake in the middle of the night with its aliveness. In the dream I was holding a huge gilded book, as in a fairy tale. Each page was thick, solid and multidimensional. Turning the two-foot-tall pages, I searched for *my page* within the sacred tome. I was looking into the *Akashic Records*. I recognized my page the moment I laid eyes on it: an immense, deep darkness illuminated only by stars. Lines of shimmering light drawn between each star formed a constellation. I understood this was the path of my destiny. I woke up. As I lay quietly, reflecting on the dream, I knew with certainty as infinite as the night sky that my life path was perfectly, mystically, and ideally mapped out before me. Infused with a profound sense of grace, I felt the deepest trust that whatever was supposed to happen next would happen with ease.

Akasha is a Sanskrit word meaning sky. The Akashic Records, what Jewish tradition calls the Book of Life, are professed to contain a vibrational record of every soul. They are an archetypal symbol for a word Lois often used: destiny. In the same way an acorn has a DNA code written inside of it to become an oak tree, I, too, had a code; in this case my soul-code. As I gazed inward to my page, I saw that the stars, and the glistening light lines between them, had deepened into infinity. I realized, *There is no final destination; the life of my soul is a never-ending, ongoing journey.* I realized that even when I take my last breath in this body, the life of my spirit would never end. *I am a work in progress; my consciousness—all consciousness—continues forever!* With this knowledge at my core, I call on the glimmering light as I move forward, understanding that legacy is the impact of all our actions, attitudes, and behaviors—the sum total of a soul's journey through life. Spirit of Resh is my legacy in progress, born from the love of my ancestors. It is the sweet fruit of my Tree of Life, and my awakening into a wholly—and holy—renewed purpose for living.

There are certain Jewish prayers I have carried since my young days of Sunday school. The benediction of the *Kaddish*, commemorating our loved ones and weaving their legacy into the tapestry of an expanded consciousness, is one of them. Together, in Temple, we'd stand to recite it in Hebrew, honoring the deceased by celebrating the Eternal. Whenever I hear the familiar Hebrew chant, *Yitgadal V'yit'kadash Shmei Rabah,* I am transported to the village hearth. Closing my eyes, I imagine the everlasting light, a symbol of the divine, which burns in every Temple. It is the heart fire at the center of our whole, extended clan. Its luminescence reaches beyond the grandmothers and toddlers, the gregarious teens and varied adults who make up the gathered clan. Beyond all stages of life, the light flickers into the ether, where it touches ancestral ghosts, lineages going back through all time. The ancient worlds entwine in a spiral dance with the Hebrew words as they are chanted in the temple of matter. People wrap their arms around one another—some weeping, others holding the hands of the bereaved. Heads are bowed or turned to the heavens. Lips move in synchrony with the rhythm while still others sit as silent witnesses to the great cycle of life. We are all one family. In this holy act of shared sorrow, I feel reassured that my loved ones live on in the heart and memory of all who still cherish their name. I whisper the names of my ancestors and reach beyond imagination to those I don't know. I sway to the chant, the ancient language reminding me that the rainbow bridge exists as the gossamer thread between worlds.

Though I found many translations of *The Mourner's Kaddish*, each celebrating the divine in its unique way, this one speaks most clearly to my heart. It is from the Jewish Renewal Movement, and I especially like how it aligns with the Siddha Yoga philosophy and with my own approach to soul and spirit:

May the Source of all being,
through our expanding awareness and our fuller action,
become more Holy.

May all the names of all the beings in the universe,
including those whom we can no longer touch,

but who have touched our hearts and lives,
and including our own selves,
live within that Source.

May its mystery live within each one of us.

May The Source of all being be blessed and celebrated,
its beauty honored and raised high.

May we praise the Source of all being in all Its Holiness.

Amen.

Celebrating the Kaddish is one of the ways I honor Dave and Lois, the rarest of birds in my tribal village. As I whisper their names in my heart...*Lois*...*Dave*...I remember Seth's words, written on a Valentine's Day card given along with a delicate gold necklace of a bird perched on a branch: "You're a rare bird, too!" Indeed, we are all rare birds. As special as Lois and Dave were, they were everyday, ordinary people like you and me. They made extraordinary choices about how to live and how to die, and so can we. My prayer is that all of you will receive my two sweet, rare birds as ancestors in your village of the heart and consider their legacy of love as your own.

Spirit of Resh is how my story of love and loss ends, but it is also the beginning of a new, unwritten chapter. I pray that it be a sanctuary in this vast, greater-than-human world. This is how I am following my star. May you find and follow yours, too.

Epilogue: Sitting Shiva

In the year following my family's deaths, I entered an extended *shiva*—the Jewish process of gathering to share food and tell stories of a loved one for seven days after their passing. Really, it's what mourners do across all cultures—gathering in community to feed more than the belly, nourishing heart and soul. Though I didn't sit formal *shiva*, I collected stories about Lois and Dave. In a virtual way my computer became the hearth of my village, where I sat and wove a tale for all of us who still grieved and needed to remember.

I invite you to *sit shiva* with me now, as a few others pick up the talking stick to share the legacy Lois and Dave left. Join me at the village hearth, to listen, to remember and to love.

Carsten Kampe, MD

As one of the many physicians Lois and Dave entrusted with their care during their cancer journey, I am deeply honored to have known them both and to have played a role in their lives. I was their local Austin oncologist and supervised much of their treatment.

An oncologist, by virtue of his profession, faces life and death on a daily basis. Nevertheless, we are never comfortable with it.

Lois and Dave were far too young and full of life to be dealt these cards. How could they possibly deal with such misfortune? How would Lois and Dave react when I would tell them of the limitations of what modern medicine had to offer them? I was sure to find two terribly depressed people. Or was I?

I struggled with these concerns and wondered how our next meetings would go. Little did I know about Lois and Dave. They had already made plans. They had already embarked on a journey—a *cancer journey*. Lois and Dave seemed, not only to have come to terms with their diagnoses; they adopted a remarkable coping strategy that they followed together, turning their terrible prognoses into a remarkable realization that "Love is everything that matters."

Lois and Dave seemed to live by that maxim. It became their motto. On most occasions—when both were healthy enough and out of the hospital—they came together for their office visits. Sure, we talked about the various treatments, progress, setbacks, side effects, and options, but we also discussed so much more: their journey together. I got to know them well. Their love for each other was obvious, as evidenced in their words, their actions, body language, and in their eyes. I remember remarking to Dave one day how inspiring their love was and how I wondered if the cancer-free world knew what they were missing. *Are they (we) missing out on finding our blue bird of happiness?*

I learned as much from them as they from me. Lois and David left a big impact in my life. Their memory remains strong. I call them up again every now and then to keep the memory alive. In the quiet of the early morning, last weekend, I spontaneously said their names out loud as if to strengthen the memory. The next day, Lois's sister Lily wrote to ask for our memories and stories of Lois and Dave (I think Lois and Dave are still speaking to us).

We are saddened and crestfallen by their passing but enriched and uplifted in having known these two rare birds of a feather who stuck together during a fantastic journey that taught us all that, indeed, Love is all that matters.

Allison Hornung:

Their love just came through in how they talked about other people, in how much they appreciated life…in how strong their faith was. It was so solid. I never heard a doubt from either one of them. "This is what God's given us to handle. We can handle it." It was amazing.

The biggest thing is: Dave showed me how I want to die. He was absolutely firm in his faith. He was not afraid of dying. There was no fear. There was a certainty. I asked him, "Will you wait for me when it's my turn?" He said yes. That meant so much to me. If there is any way he can keep that promise, he will. That brings me a great sense of peace. Knowing there is someone to help me pass.

Carla Portnoy

I first met Lois and Dave about seven years ago at Southwest Regional Cancer Center. I am an oncology pharmacist and I co-facilitated a support group for patients and their families. I first heard Lois and Dave's story before I met them. My goodness, what a story! It was so unbelievable to me. How could this disease have hit them both so hard and seemingly without mercy? Then I met them for the first time in the flesh. Why were they able to exude such peaceful serenity? What was their secret? I always was a little bit anxious during group discussions, but when Lois and Dave were present at our group, my heart slowed down – I was calm and happy. I knew that anytime they were part of our discussion, it was going to be enlightening. I think they had that effect on everyone. They often called me with questions and they were so appreciative of my time and advice. But…isn't it strange that I felt as if I should be thanking them instead? Thank you Dave! Thank you Lois! What a blessing I have received by knowing them both.

Lanie Tankard:

I first met Lois and Dave at a cancer support group meeting the year my husband Jim was diagnosed with stage-four lung cancer. Over the next five years, Jim and I attended as many of these meetings as we could, connecting with others traveling the same path. We bolstered each other up—all of us in awe of Dave and Lois, who each played both patient and caregiver roles.

Jim and I connected with their courage, their intelligence, and their obvious love for one another. They looked right into your very soul when they talked to you, yet we also drew strength from their lighthearted, witty, and downright honest approach to cancer.

Whenever Jim or Lois or Dave was in the hospital for whatever reason, we always visited each other but a weekend retreat sponsored by the American Cancer Society is where we really bonded. We were joined by our three daughters and the seven of us spent the weekend doing tai chi, art, canoeing, hiking, stargazing, and relaxing in the pool.

When Jim began hospice care Dave and Lois came several times to visit. They sat with him, Lois rubbing his back, and Dave talked directly about what was ahead. Dave was never afraid to skirt the tough topics, doing so with a keen insight and purity that resonated. We all thought the world of both of them.

Jim died in August 2005, during a typically hot Austin summer. The last time they visited, Lois wanted to chat with me in the den in order to let Dave and Jim visit. She propped my feet in her lap and told me to lean back and relax while she gave me a soothing foot massage and I left my worries behind for a few minutes. I hadn't realized how much I'd needed to unwind, but she had a sixth sense about such matters.

We walked back into the living room to find Jim fast asleep on the couch, with Dave nowhere in sight. Suddenly I caught a movement out the window, and there was Dave, watering our parched brown lawn in a desperate effort to keep something around the place alive. To comply with Austin watering restrictions, he had to stand there, on that hot August day, holding the garden hose in his hand. He had beads of sweat running down his cheeks and a peaceful smile on his face. I looked at Lois, and she at me, and the droplets that ran down our cheeks were not sweat. We hugged, bonded forever in whatever form our souls take. I'm sure Jim is thoroughly enjoying their company now and I, too, still sense them from time to time...

More stories may be found at www.tworarebirds.org

Food for Thought: A reader's guide

Metaphorical Death:

Both Sally and Lily talk about death in a metaphorical way. In the Foreword, Sally says, "We each die many deaths in one lifetime. We die to childhood and enter adolescence, then die to adolescence as we become adults, and we die to relationships and start new ones." Later, Lily says, "I'm able to see that the violent tearing between us was a necessary death—one without which a new beginning would have never been possible." Eventually Lily comes to understand that "One must pass through death in order to be transformed."

- What do the sisters mean when they use the word *death* in this context?
- As the family faces literal death(s), are there any metaphorical deaths they encounter?

Literal Death:

Lily was scared to be the first to say that it was ok for her dad to die, then took a breath and said, "You've lived a long life; it's ok with me if you go." Later, when he died, she cheered as Lois cried.

- What does Lily's anxiety suggest about the culture's relationship to death?
- What would you do in a similar situation?
- Why did Lily cheer when her dad passed?

When Lois said, "I don't know how to die." Lily's response was, "I think it has to do with surrender."

- What do you think she meant by that? Surrender to *what?*
- What does surrender mean to you?
- How did Lois and Dave's way of engaging with their pending deaths inform the way they lived?

Wounding:

Lily said "I think about how wounds are passed down from one generation to the next, through both nature and nurture." She then goes on to explore her ancestral patterns by saying, "...I've often wondered whether their experience of persecution created the perpetrator and victim consciousness in our DNA. *Did Lois and I, in our close relationship, pick up those patterns?* Without a single doubt, Lois and I loved each other, but that did not stop us from projecting our wounds onto one another."

- What does Lily mean by "...projecting our wounds onto one another?"
- What does *picking up an ancestral pattern* mean?
- How do ancestral patterns (from both maternal and paternal lineages) appear in Lily and Lois's lives? What about in Dave's life? What about in their relationships?
- Have you inherited any patterns from your ancestors?

Wounding and wholeness:

When Lily wakes in the night with the phrase, *It is ones wholeness that causes one to seek wholeness*, she says, "The fall does not symbolize original sin, as it is often interpreted. It is symbolic of the original wound of all humanity. All of us, in whatever form, however consciously or unconsciously, are seeking a return to that existential home."

- How do *you* interpret the phrase, "it is ones wholeness that causes one to seek wholeness?"
- Lily reinterprets the concept of *original sin* into one of *original wounding*. Does that reframe your understanding of the story's meaning? If so, how?
- What do the words, *existential home*, mean to you?

Healing & Forgiveness:

After Lily and Lois sat on the couch and discussed how they'd been hurt by one another, Lily wrote, "This time she listened. She asked questions, and it felt good to be heard." Then, "Lois and I wanted to be free of the hurts that had passed between us, and I knew that forgiveness was the key to that freedom." Later Lily said, "Healthier than holding back, truth telling was building a new foundation, brick by shaky brick. It took more than a decade to build, but we'd begun crafting it with deep honesty that day on the couch."

- How did Lois and Lily's encounter on the couch contribute to their healing?
- What role did forgiveness play and what enabled them to forgive?
- What comes up for you as you consider forgiveness?
- What did Lily mean when she said that truth telling was healthier than holding back?

Love:

Lois's revelation on the operating table was a significant part of her journey. She said, "I remember the feeling of love all around me and realized that the universe was *made of love.*" Lily explained that "*Love is all that matters* became her mantra...."

- What happened to Lois while under anesthesia, and where did her revelation come from?
- How did Lois's repetition and commitment to "love is all that matters" change her life and the lives of those around her?

Gratitude

Thank you to my village, spread far and wide, for your unequivocal support of Two Rare Birds. You are the heart-fire which burns brightly at the center of my wheel. To The Symington Foundation and Richard and Grenda David, I extend a wholehearted and hearty thank you; you totally know why.

To supporters, Vivy, Leslie, Nate, Lu, Judy and Ed, Michael and Carol, Royce and Doug, Terry, Deborah, Patricia, Sally, Skye, Philip and Adele, Anna, David and Corina, Larry, Annie, Judi and Michael, Tina, Dawn, Mary, Sandy and Arina, Hallie, Diana and Art, Randi and Adam, Matt and Monique, Arnie and Barb, Adrienne and Don, and Lauren: your financial support made it possible for me to dive into Two Rare Birds full time. Thank you from the bottom of my heart!

To Patricia Britt, thank you for knowing that this book needed to be written and for reading every single excruciating rendition. To my soul-sister, Tina Benson, your belief in me helped keep my fingers to the keyboard; I am grateful for that and so much more. Much gratitude to readers Peggy, Marcy, Nefretete, Charley,

Michael, Julie, Lu, Royce, Bob and Seth for your feedback; it helped shape the story and your enthusiastic responses helped me believe in myself.

To Sally, for being born as my sister and holding your corner of the triangle with divine perfection and eternal gratitude, for your uncompromising support, for walking through the fire with me, and for your love, I bow to the vision and heart you bring to my life.

To Martha Kay Nelson, my editor-in-chief and friend-in-heart, thank you just isn't enough. For seeing the story that I most needed to tell, for holding me in a safe nest as you challenged me to deeper honesty and writing-rigor, and for chirp-chirping through three overhauls and countless re-writes, my gratitude is endless.

And last, but furthest from least, to Seth, thank you for all of it: for walking through life with me, for sitting beside me at the hearth, for your unbelievable patience, for your devotion to what matters most and for being a mate to my soul. While your appearances in this story appear fleeting, it's only because you already live so far inside me that I couldn't find many words beyond *I love you*.

About the Author

For thirty years, Lily Myers Kaplan has guided hundreds of people to navigate life's challenges, overcome traumas, and deepen spirituality, helping them become more vitally alive. Kaplan holds a master's degree in culture and spirituality from The Sophia Center of Holy Names College, but her most valued credential is her experience of living a soul-path grounded in the everyday world. Foundational to her work is a love of the natural world, a value for service, a belief that life is enhanced by embracing death, and a commitment to creating meaning and purpose as a form of healing. Kaplan currently resides in Oakland, California, with her beloved husband and their sweet dog, Shayna (which, in Yiddish, means *Beauty.)* She can be reached through her website: www.reshfoundation.org